"Global Doodle Gems" Halloween Collection Volume 3

Coverart drawn & colored Rover Hsiao

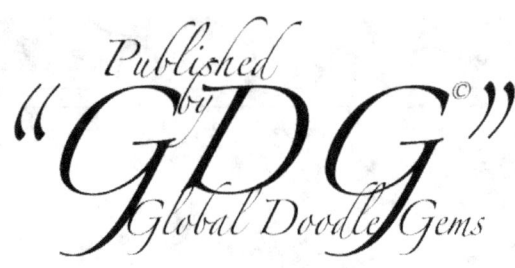

Share your colored versions with us ! We love seeing your results and hearing from you we are social !

The Official FB book page, stay on top of what we have in the works !
www.facebook.com/globaldoodlegems
The Community group, share your colored pages, meet the artists, enjoy exclusive freebies, take part in community Charity books and so much more......
www.facebook.com/groups/globaldoodlegems/
Follow us on Twitter.... @GlobalDoodlegem
We are on Instagram too
@globaldoodlegems for instagram
...and if you are not social like that we have a blog
globaldoodlegems.wordpress.com

Copyright © 2016 Global Doodle Gems
All rights are reserved by Global Doodle Gems.
Duplication of pages for personal use are allowed. You are invited to color the pages then scan/post your coloured versions to social networks, mentioning the book title and author/artist (Global Doodle Gems).
All artwork and images are protected by copyright laws. This book or any portion thereof may not, otherwise, be reproduced and/or distributed or transmitted without the express written permission of the artist/publisher of Global Doodle Gems.
All of us from the Global Doodle Gems wish you a colortastic time and look forward to seeing your wonderful color results online !

Contributing Artists

Laurie Beauchamp
Lynni Ex Doodles
Johanna Ans
Arianne Schimmel
Peggy Sue Karunding
Audrey Sagh
Alfred E. Villanueva
Maria Wedel
Carol Mayer
Charlotte Fischer
Jenny Wei
Jodi Ho
Lilan Chen
Nancy43
Pajun Chen
Pica Wu
Rover Hsiao
Wen Kung

Contributing Artist
Laurie Beauchamp
USA

Facebook : Lauries-Art

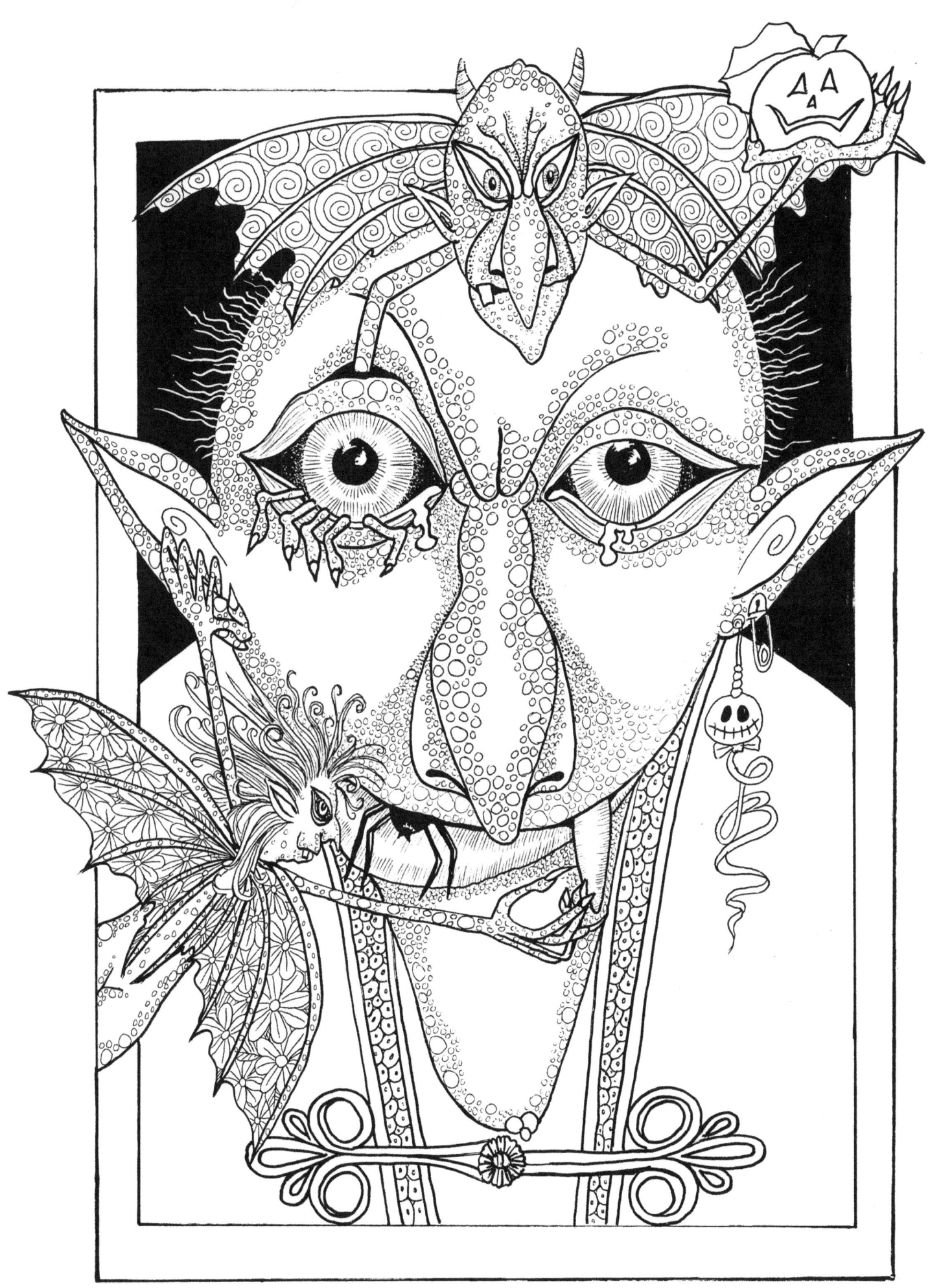

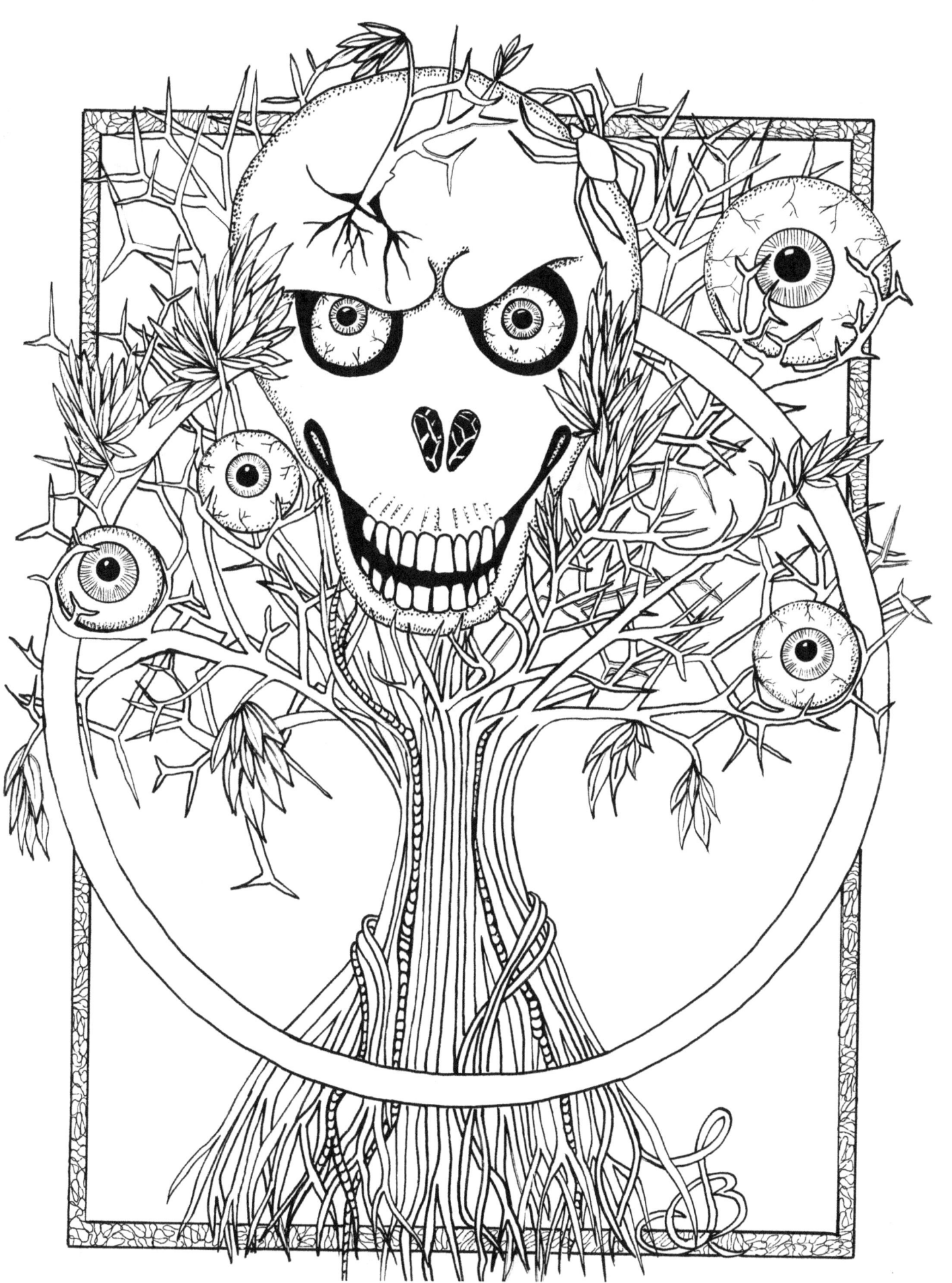

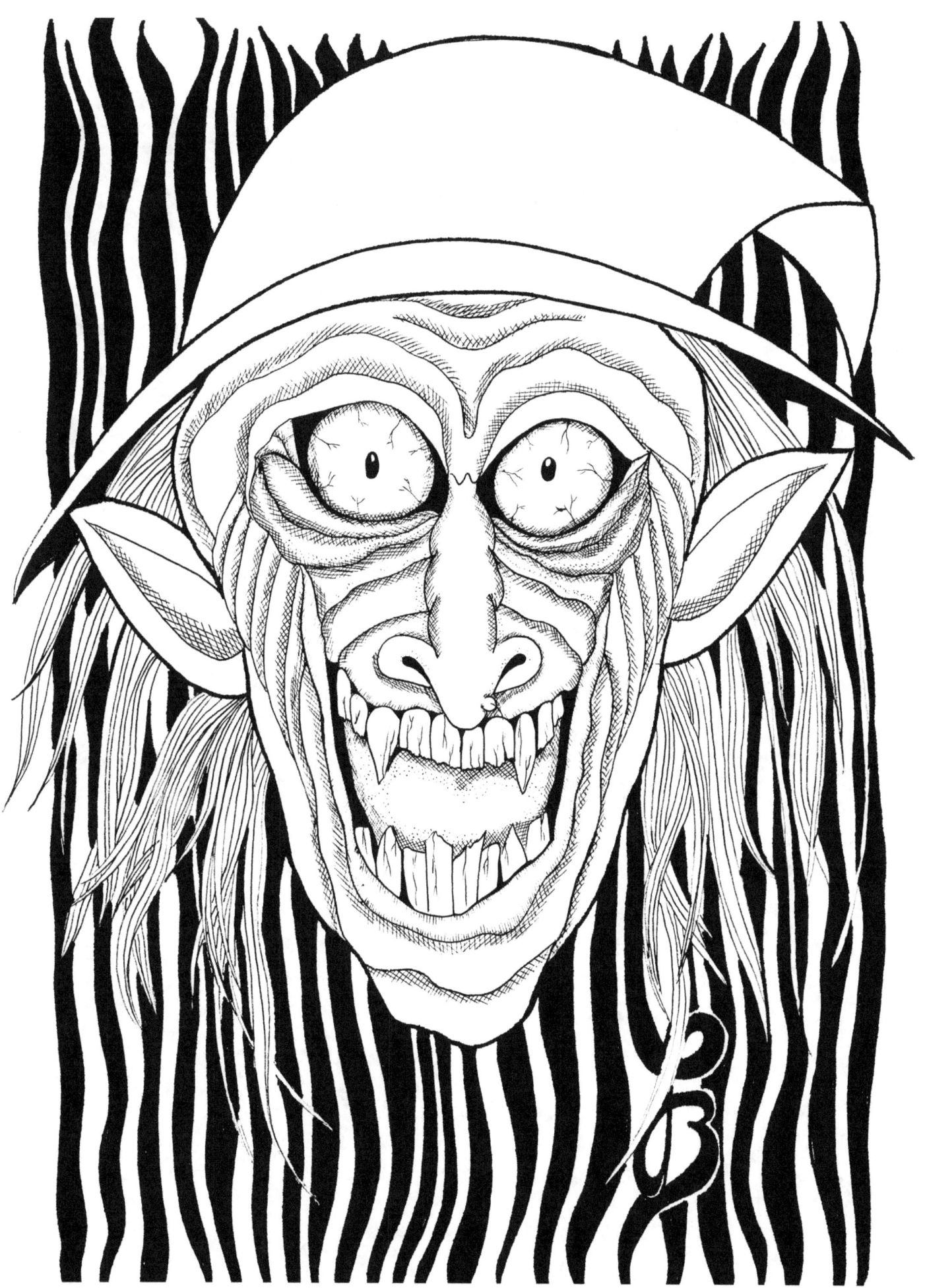

Contributing Artist
Lynniex Doodles
England

Facebook : Lynniex Doodles

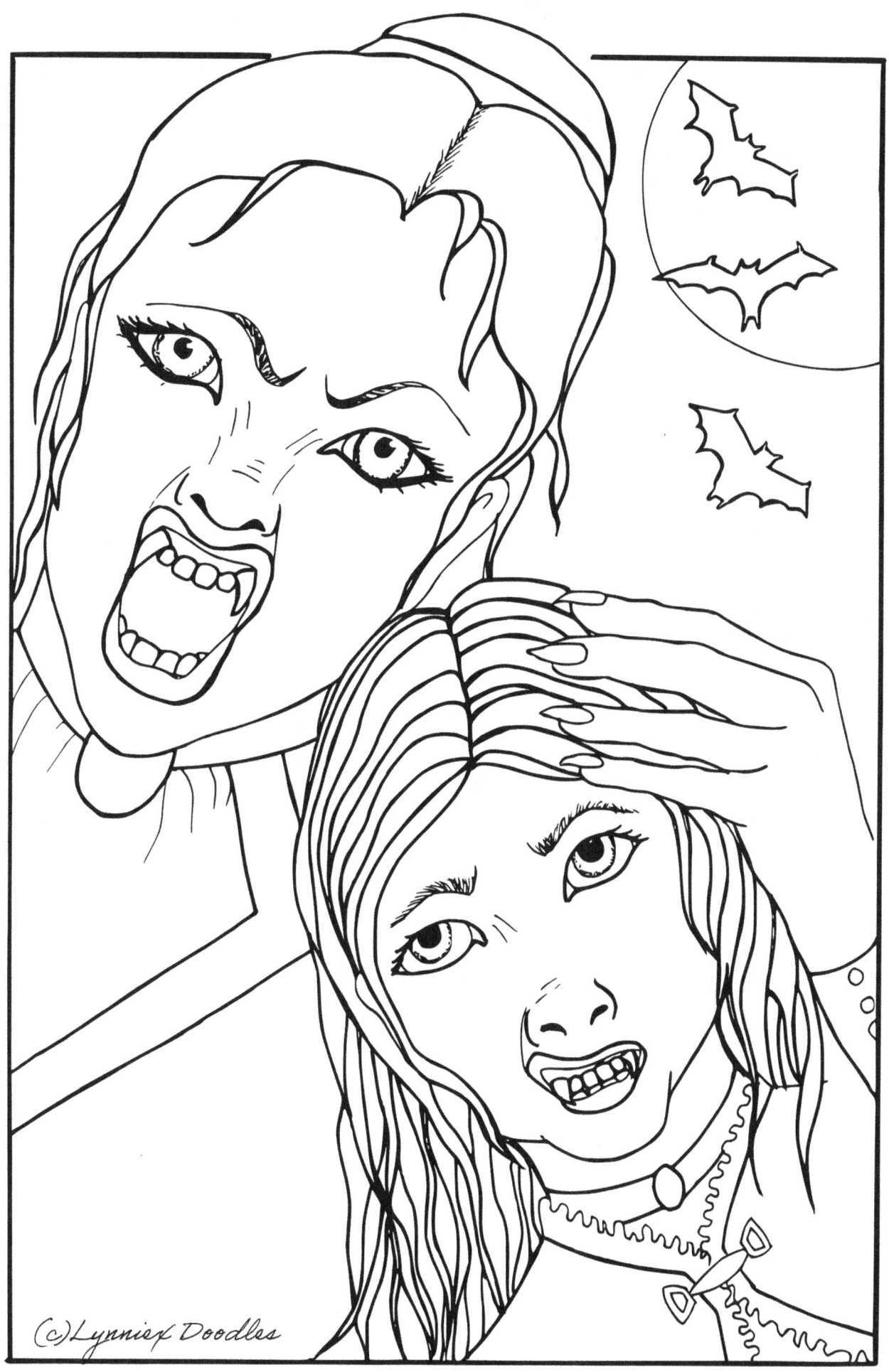

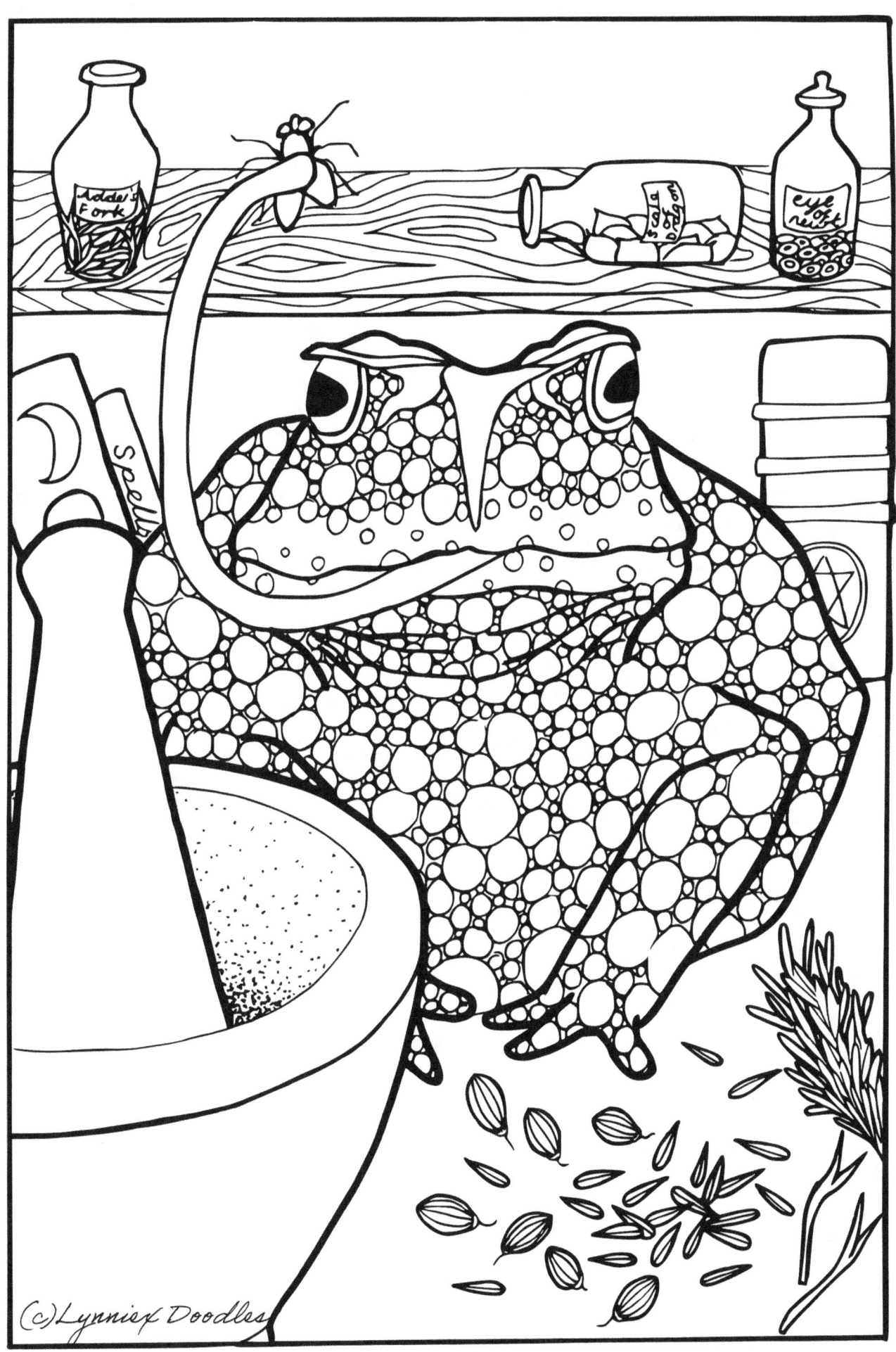

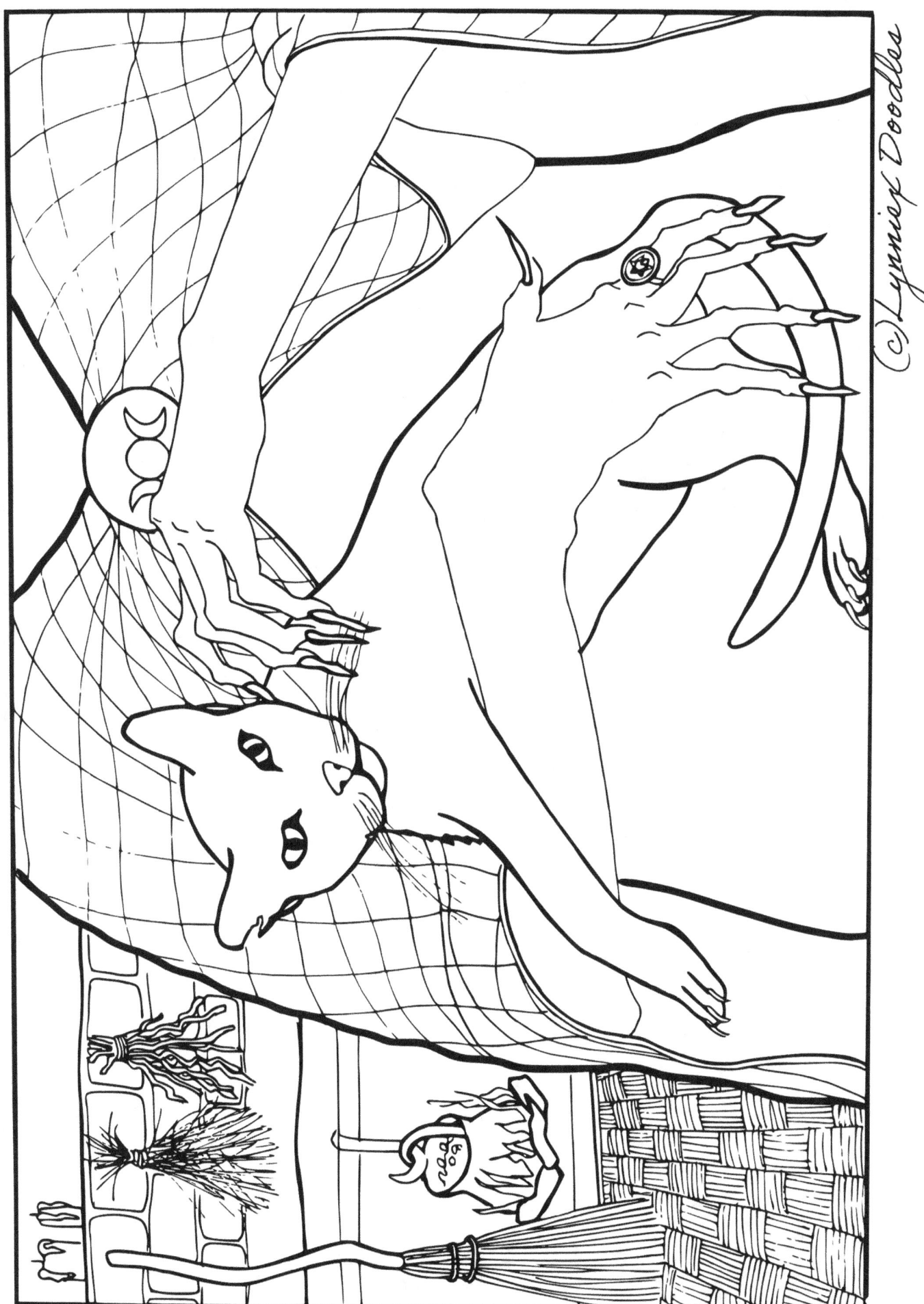

*Contributing Artist
Johanna Ans
The Netherlands*

Facebook : JohannaAns

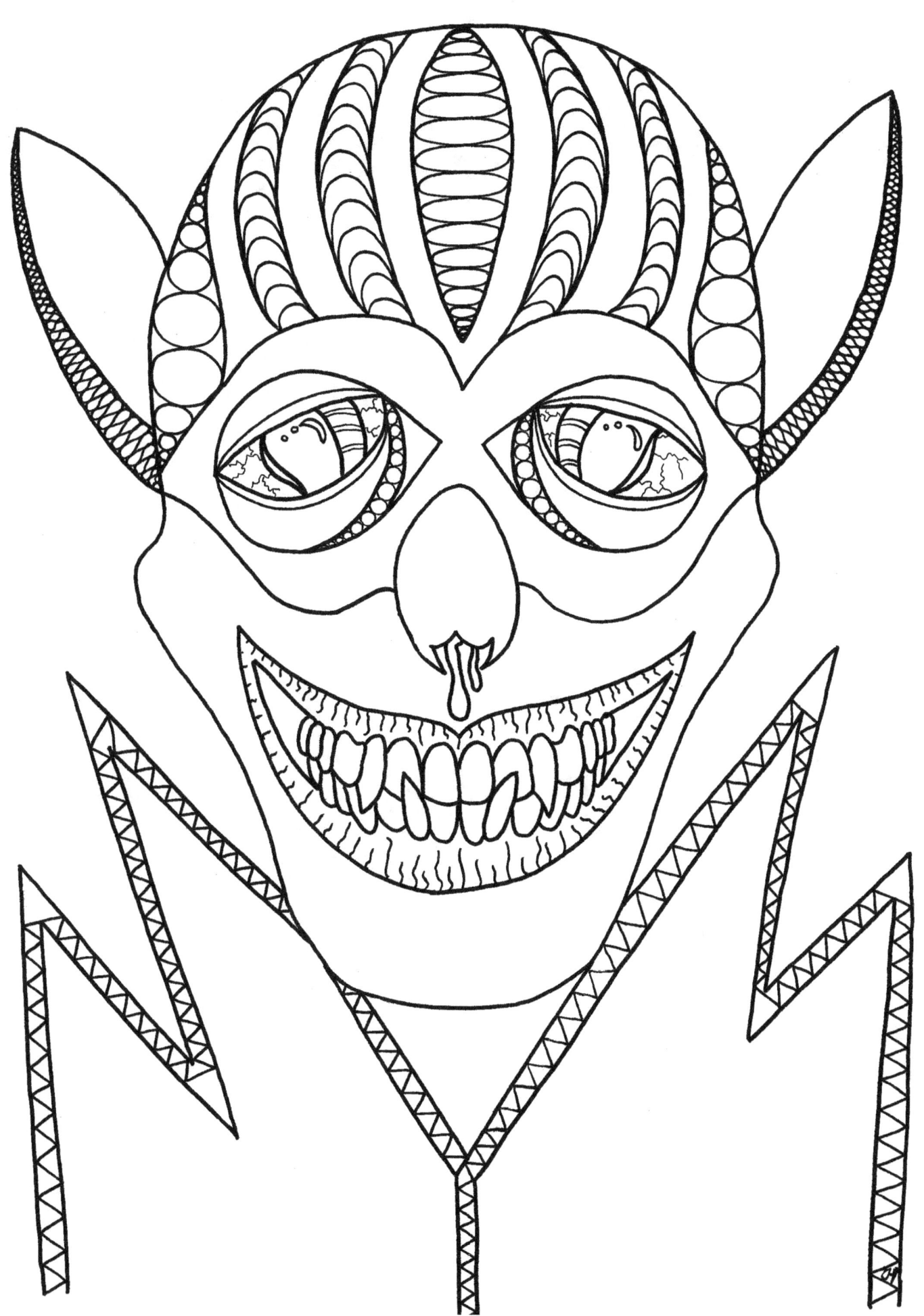

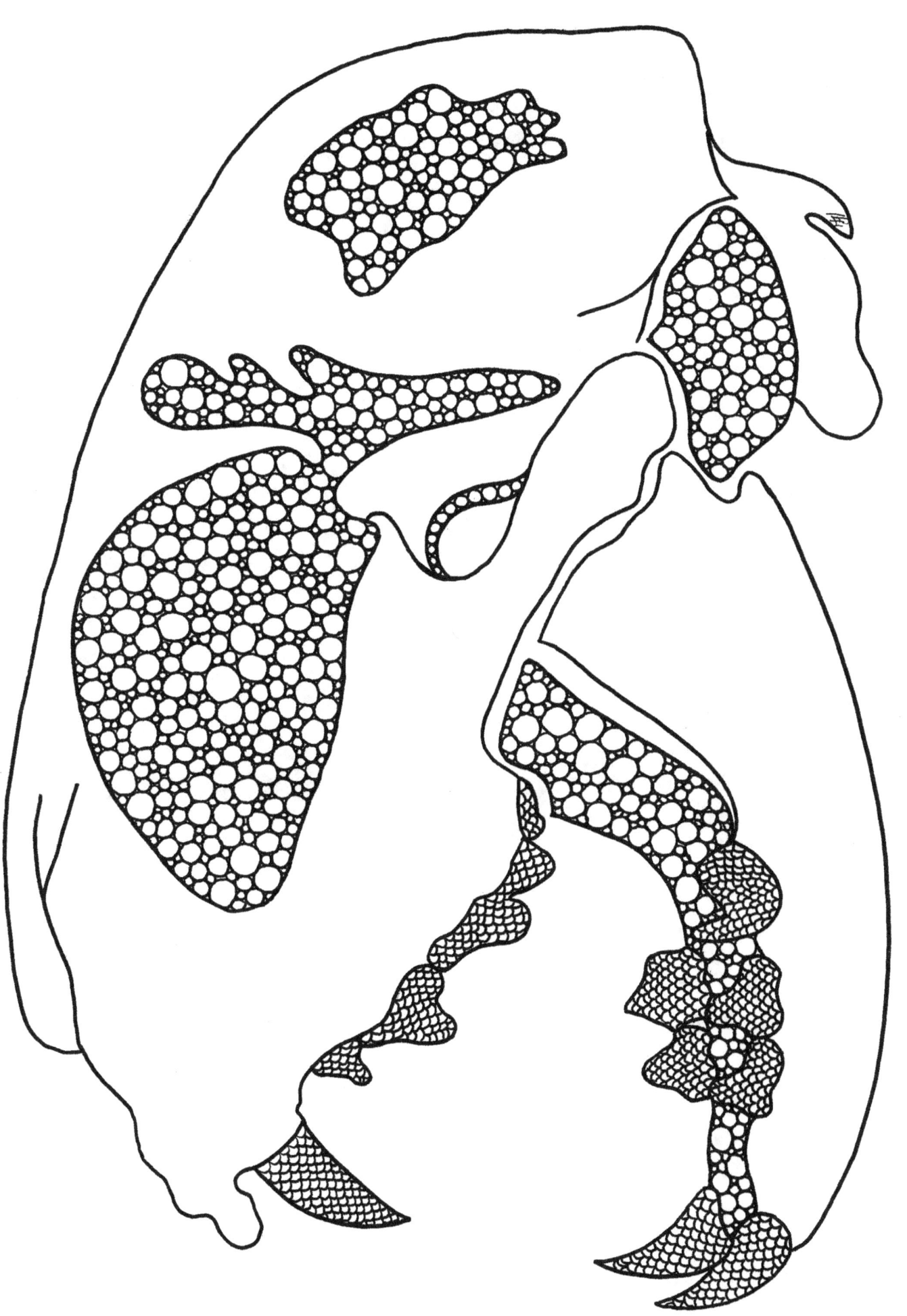

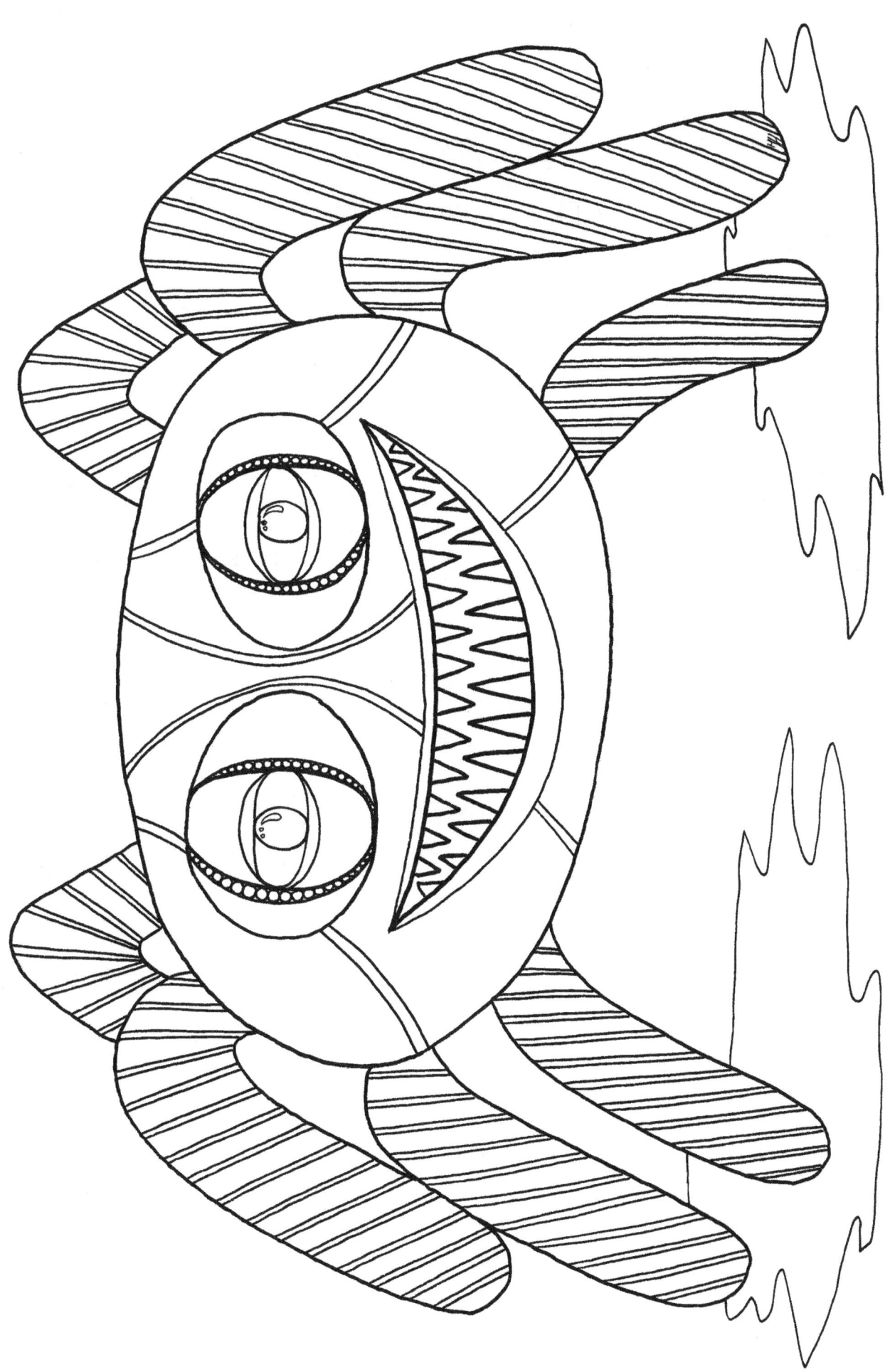

Contributing Artist
Arianne Schimmel
The Netherlands

Facebook : ArianneSchimmel

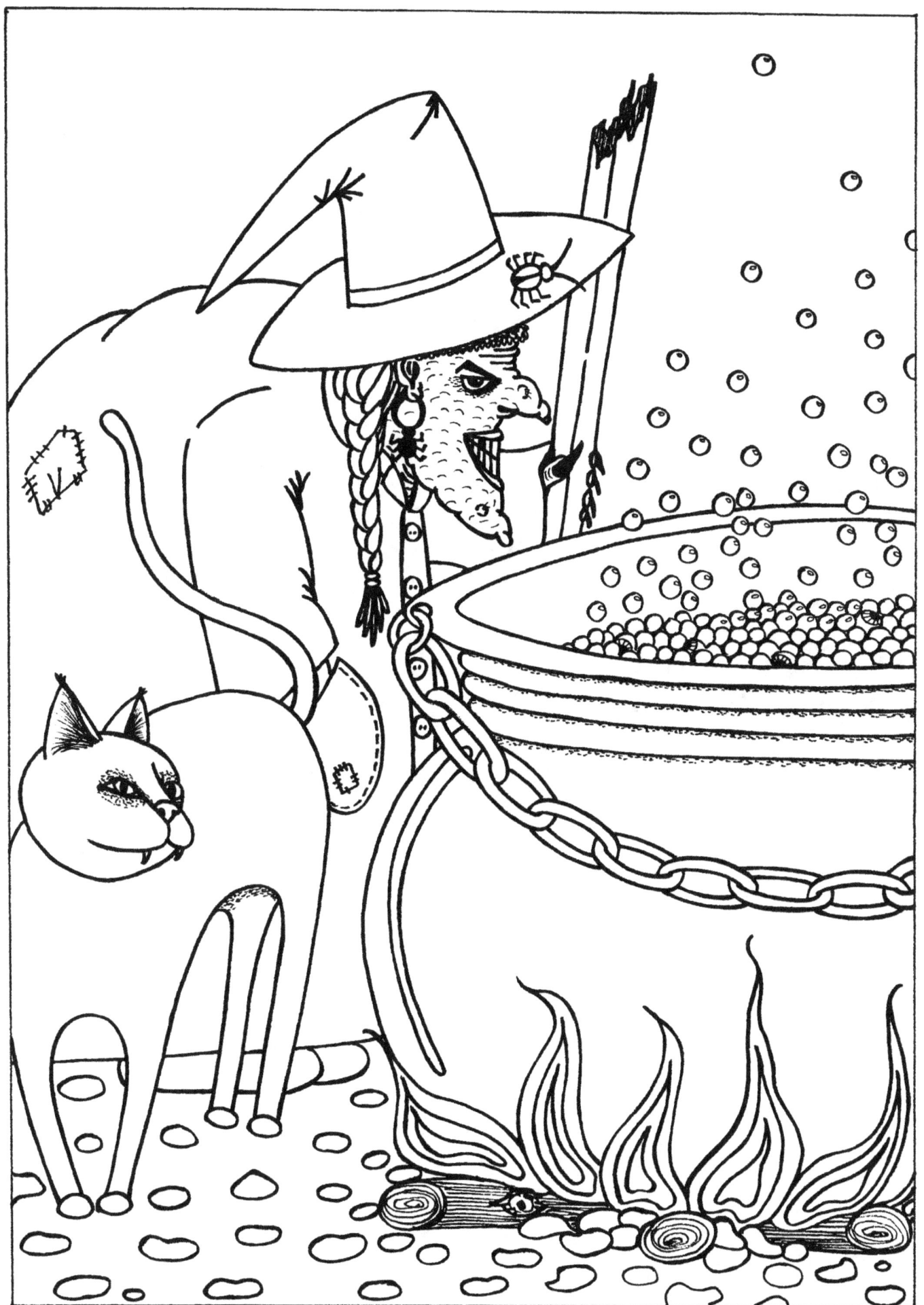

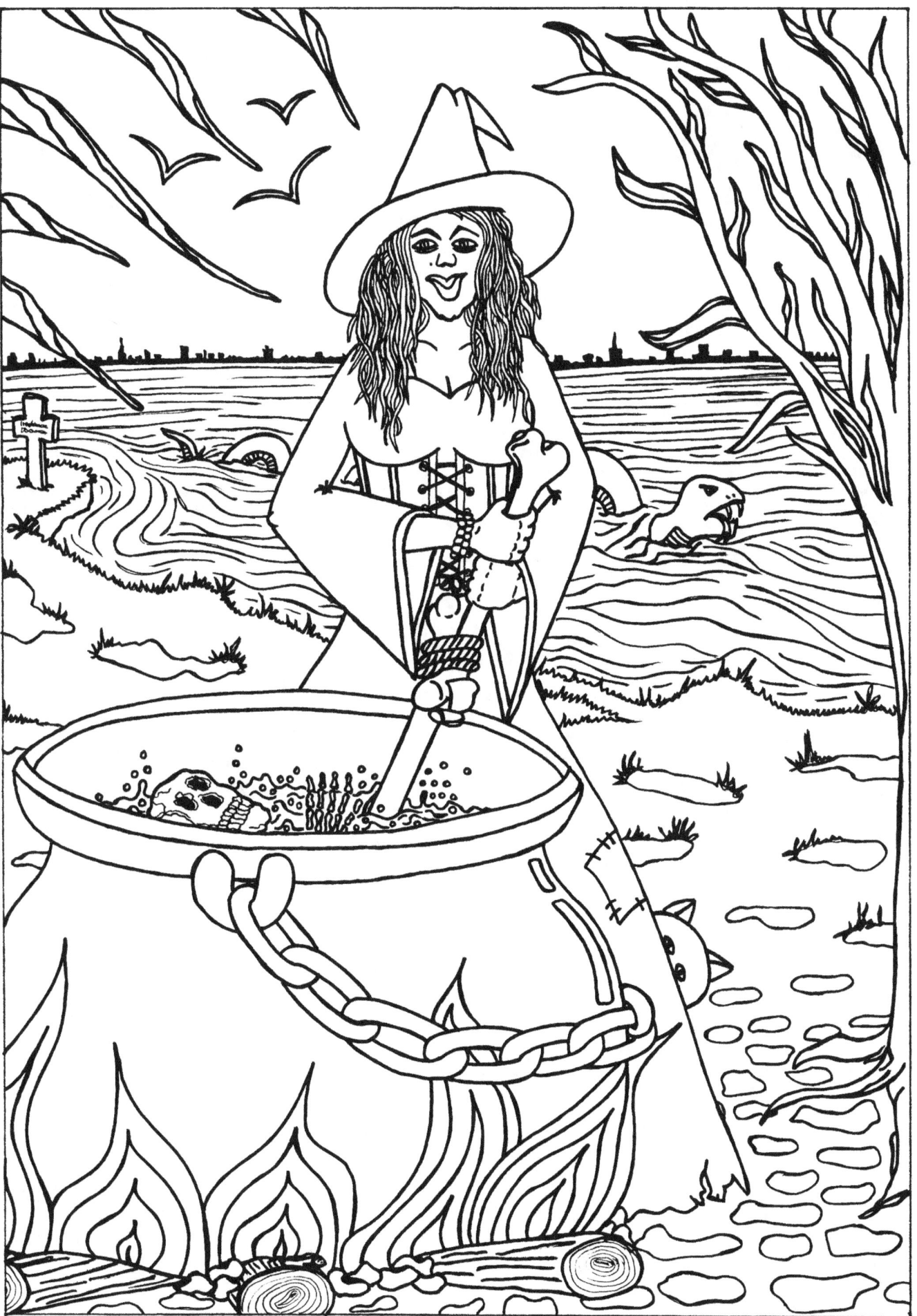

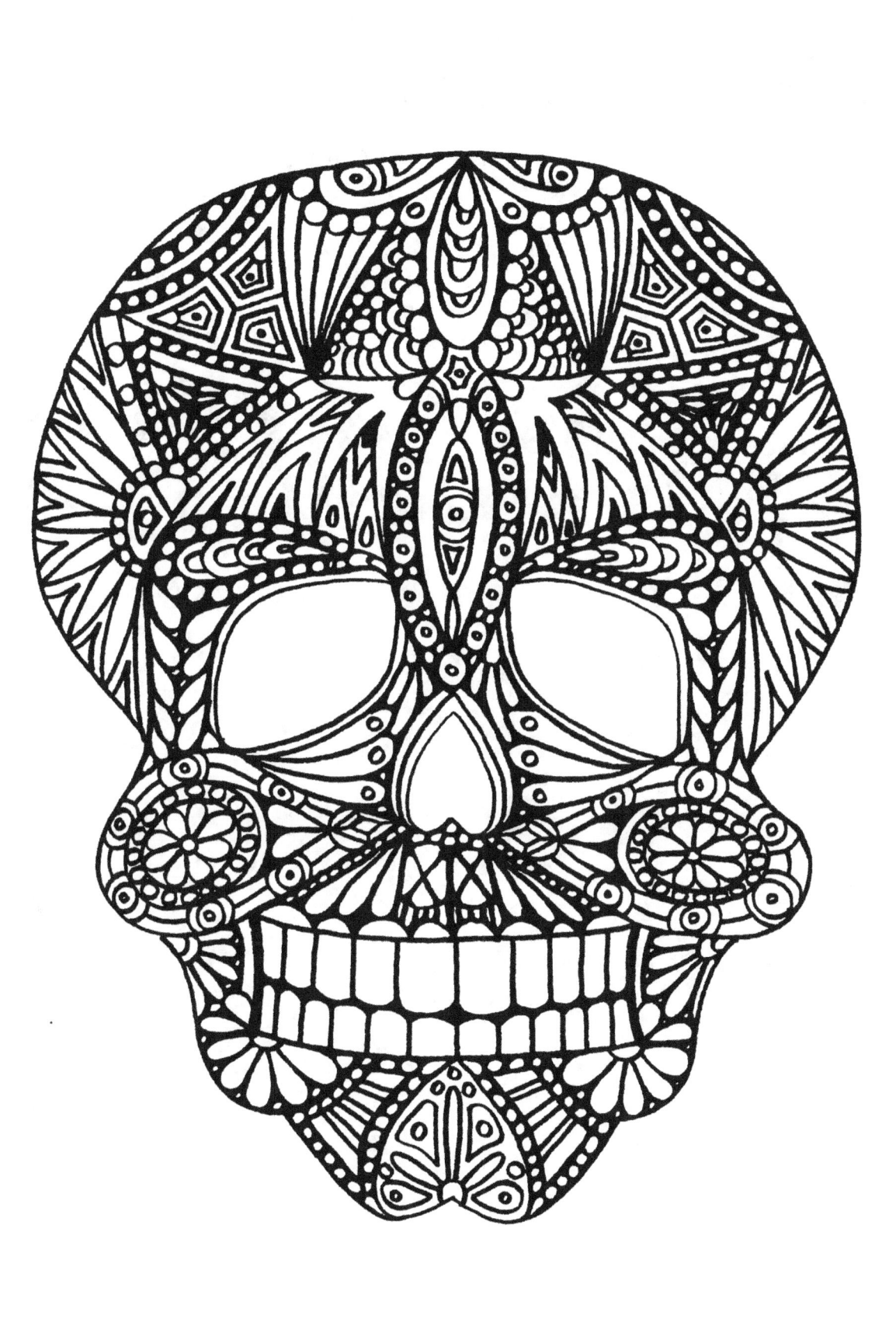

Contributing Artist
Peggy Sue Karunding
The Netherlands

Facebook : Peggy-Sues-Artwork

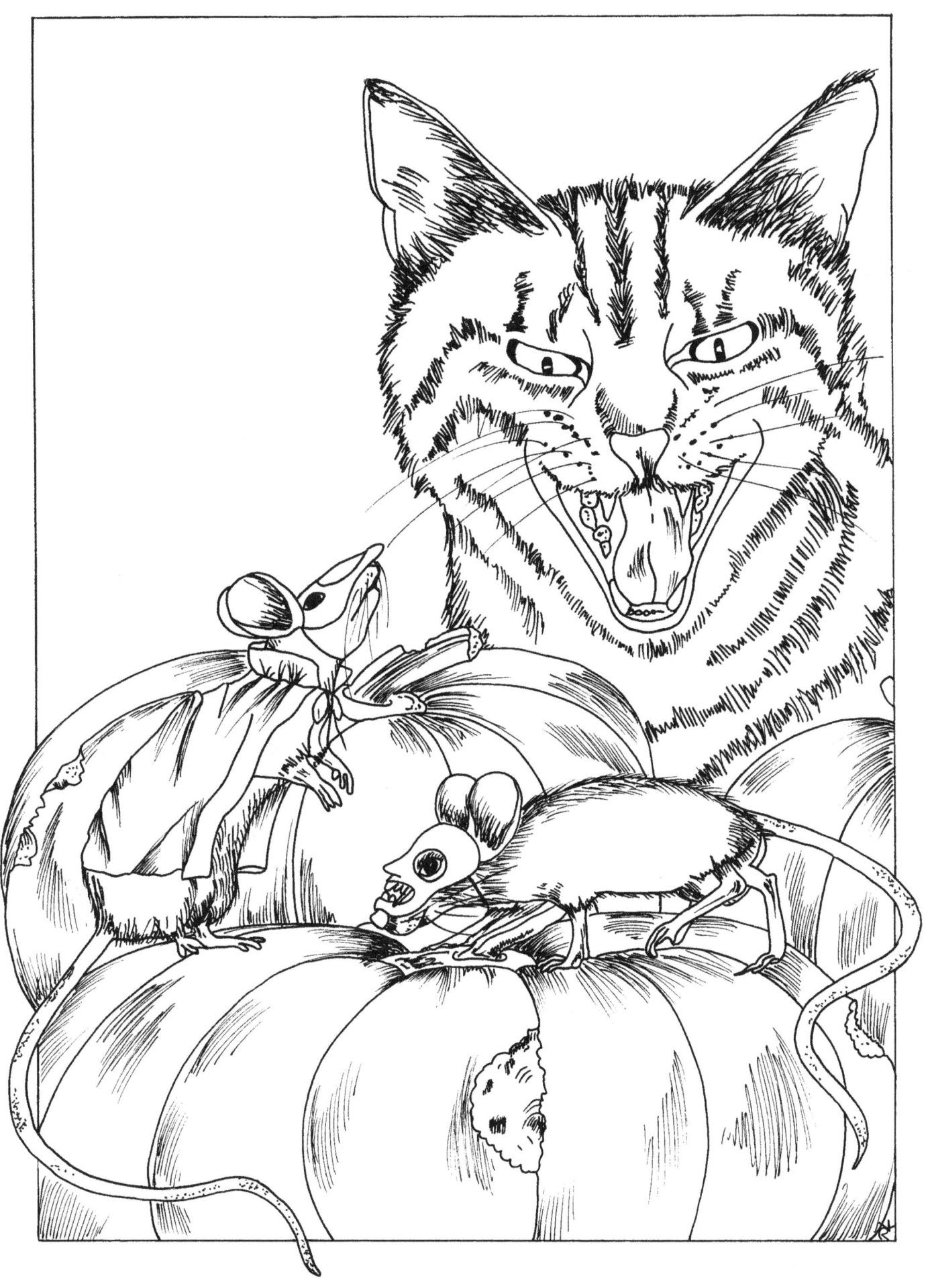

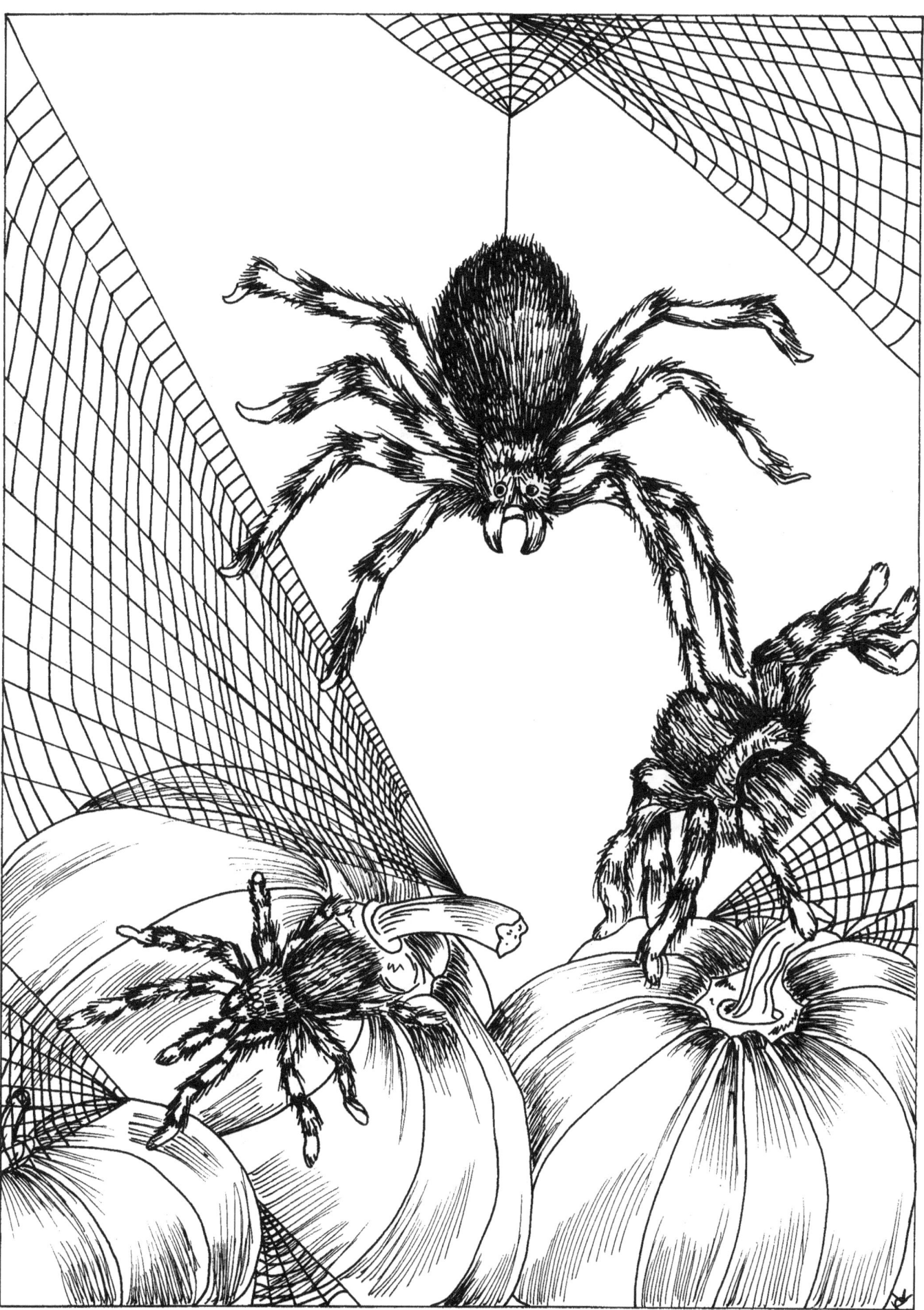

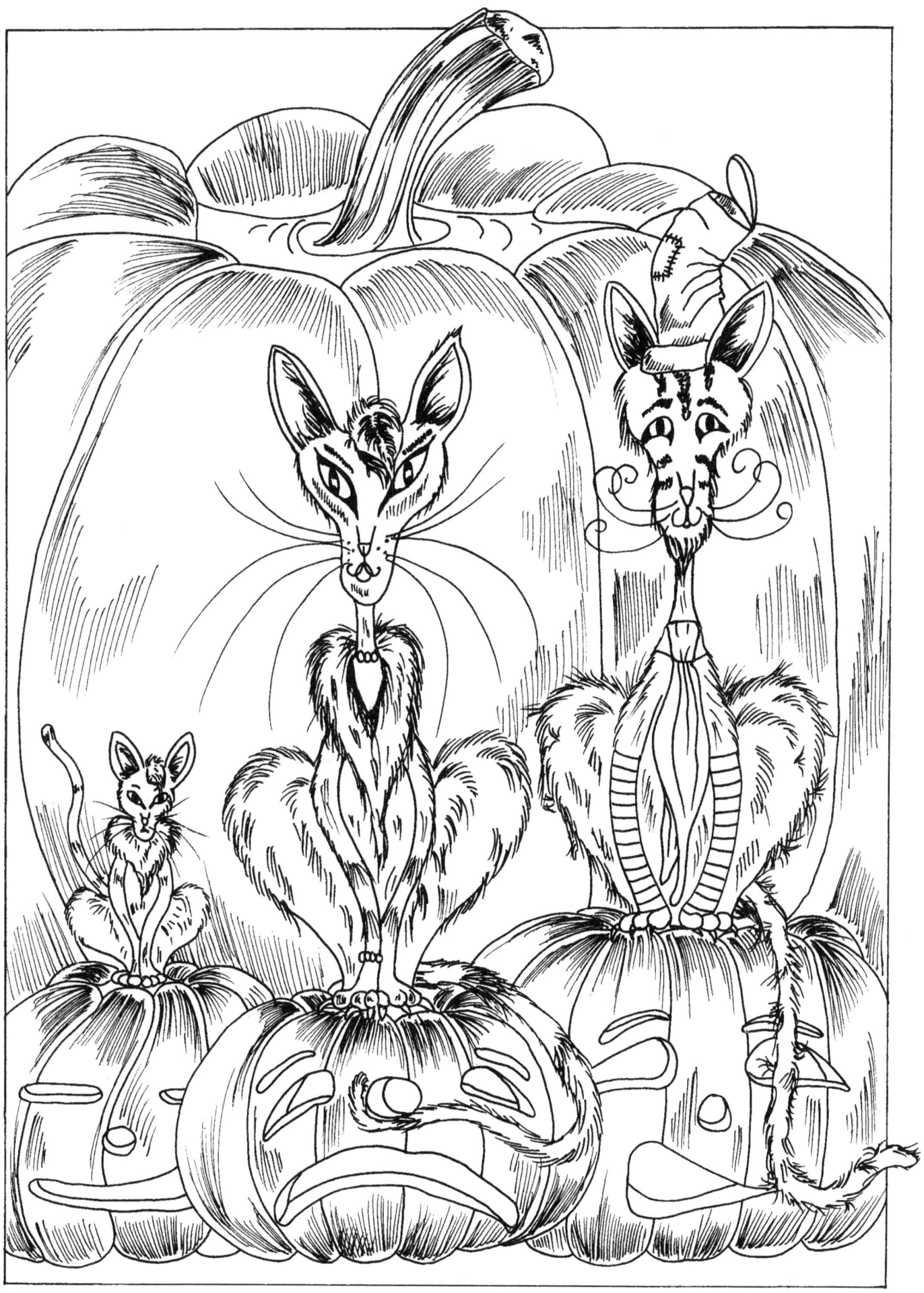

Contributing Artist
Audrey Sagh
Saskatoon, Saskatchewan Canada

Facebook : AMS-Artwork

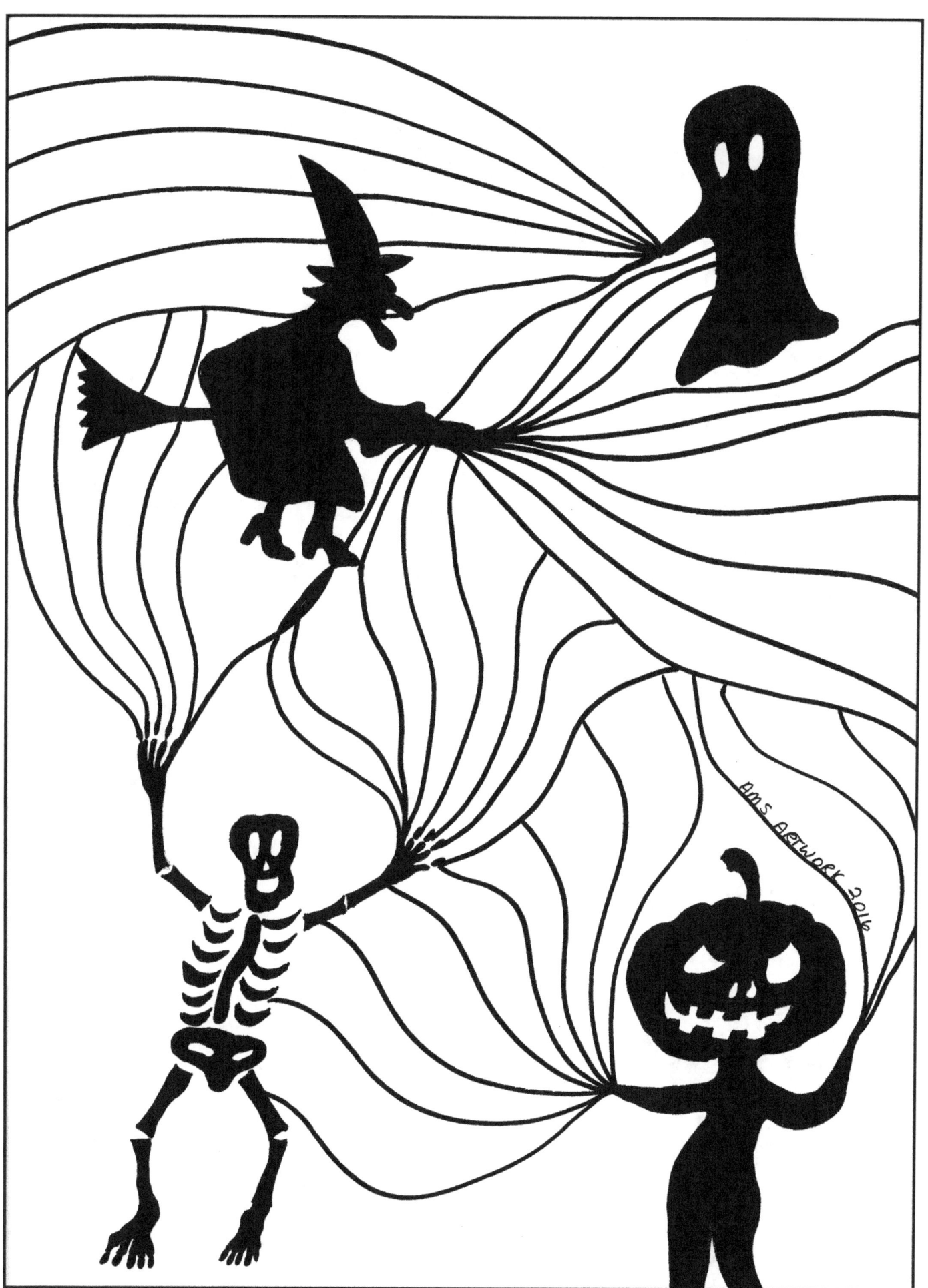

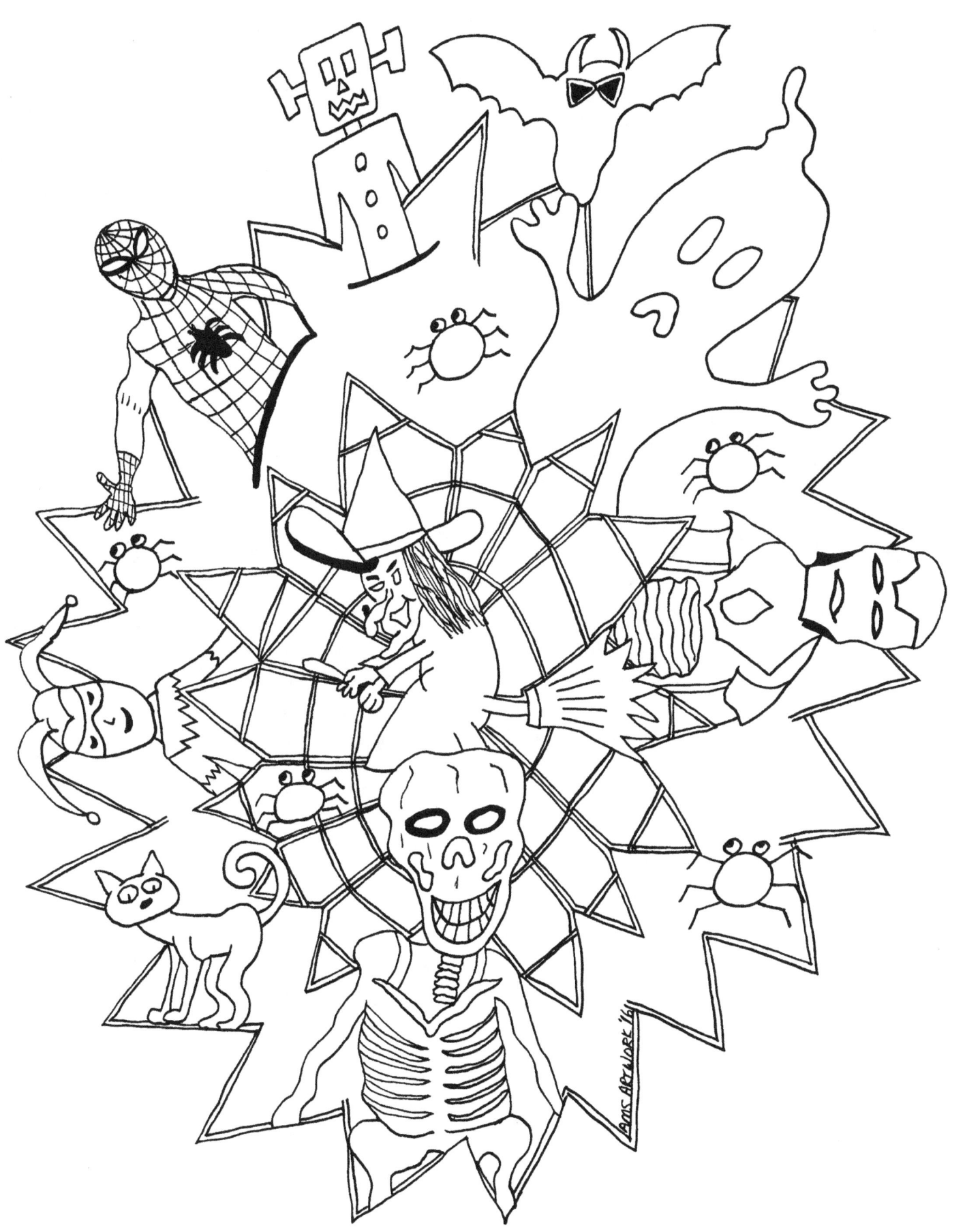

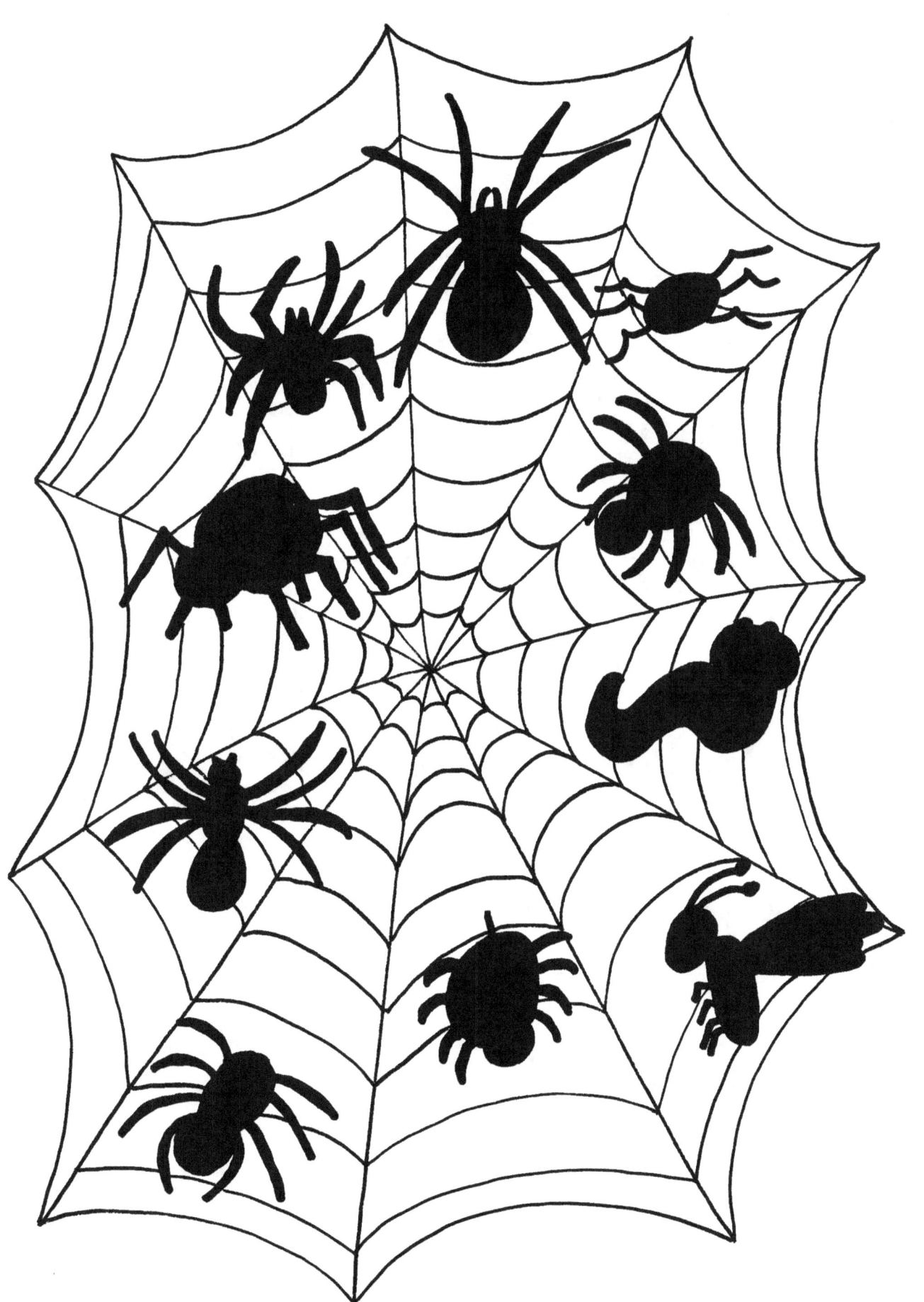

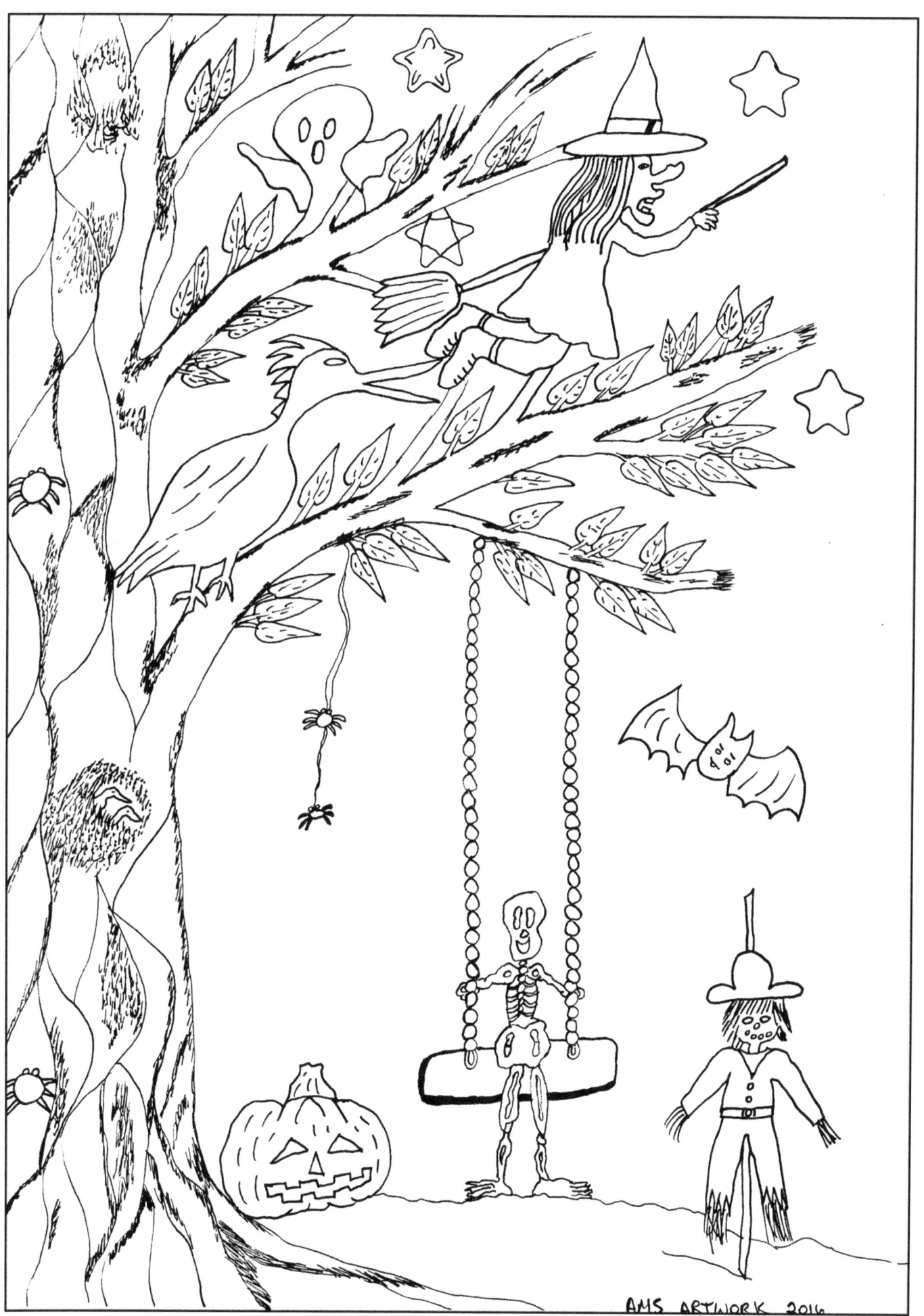

Contributing Artist
Alfred E. Villanueva
Philippines
Facebook : viworksart2015

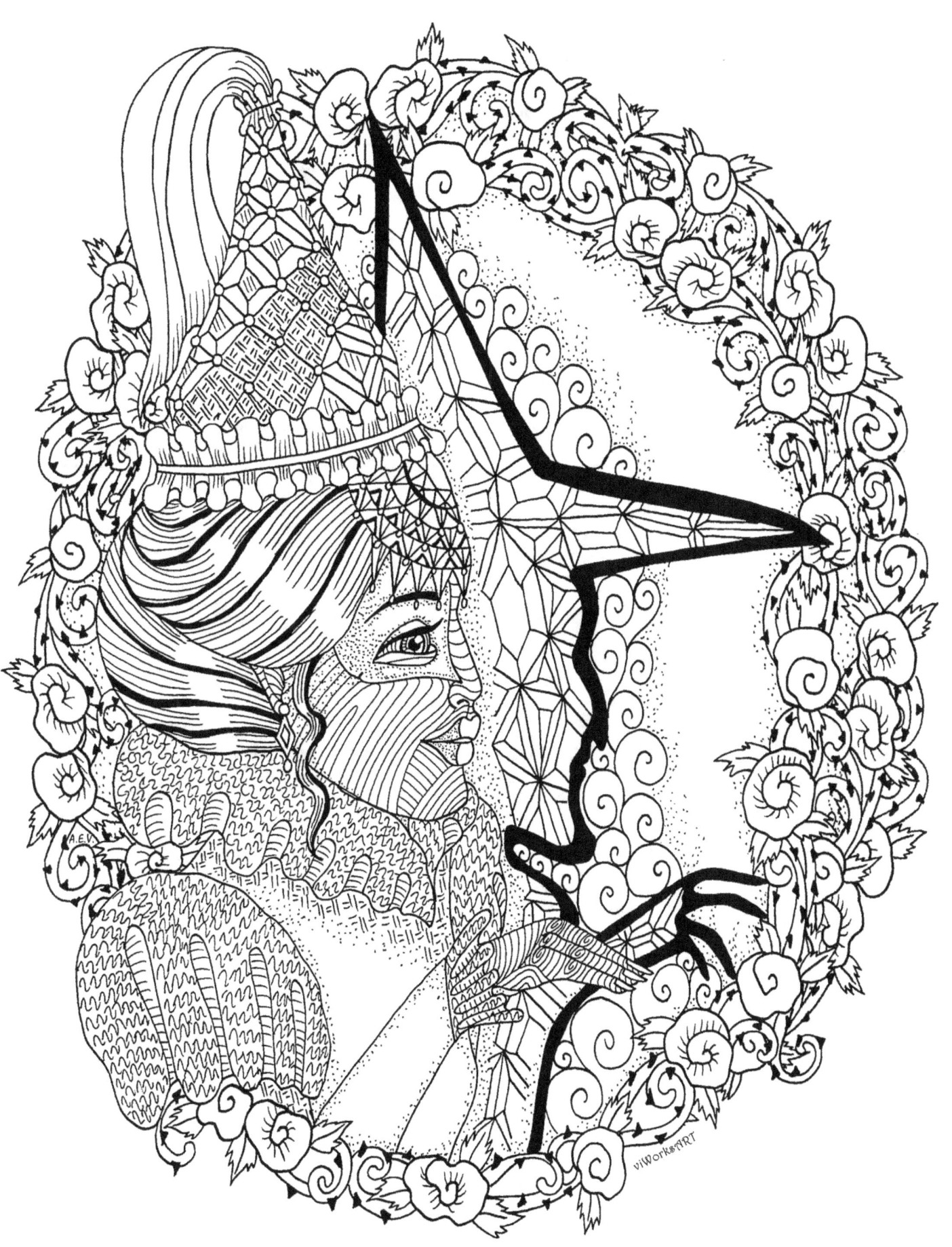

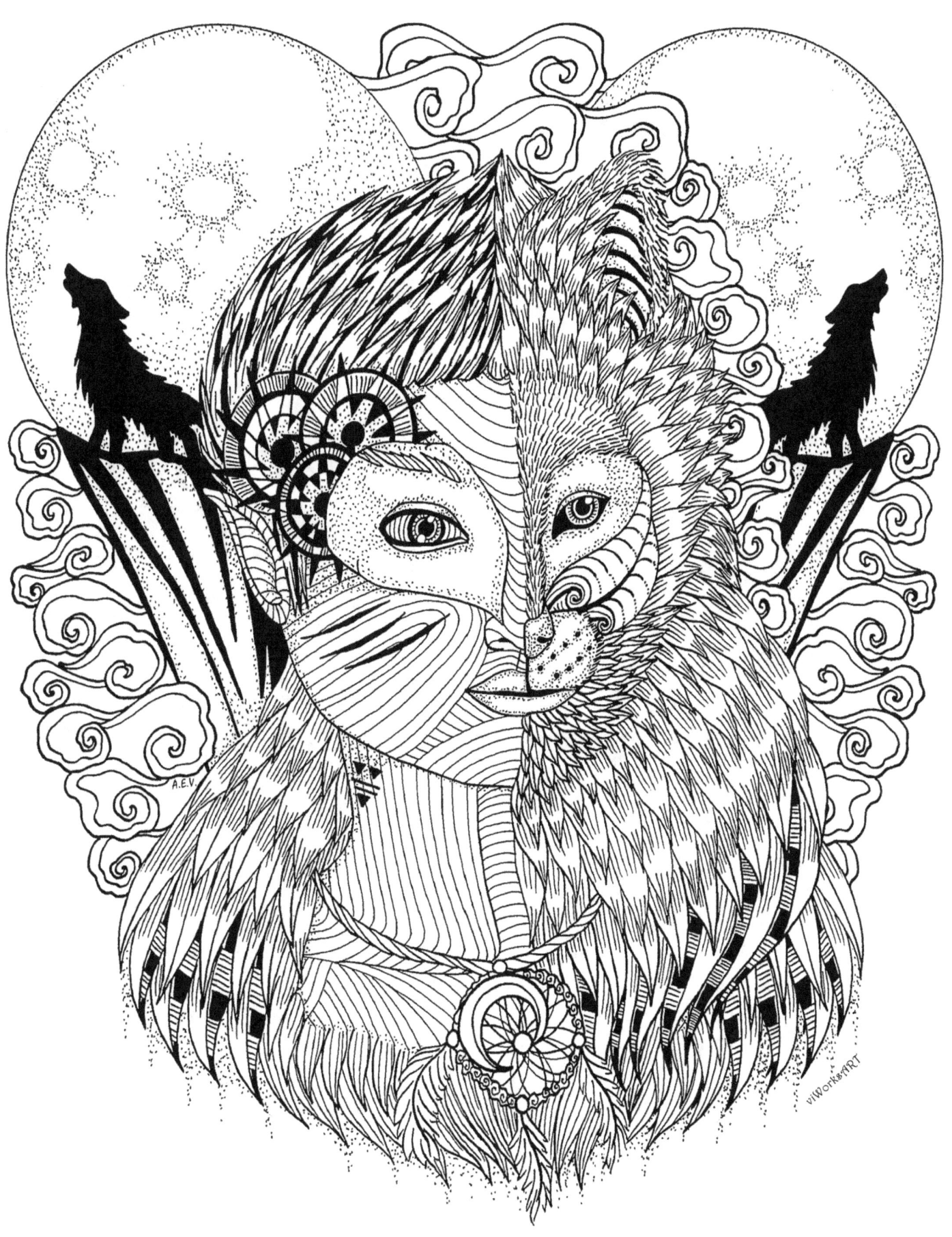

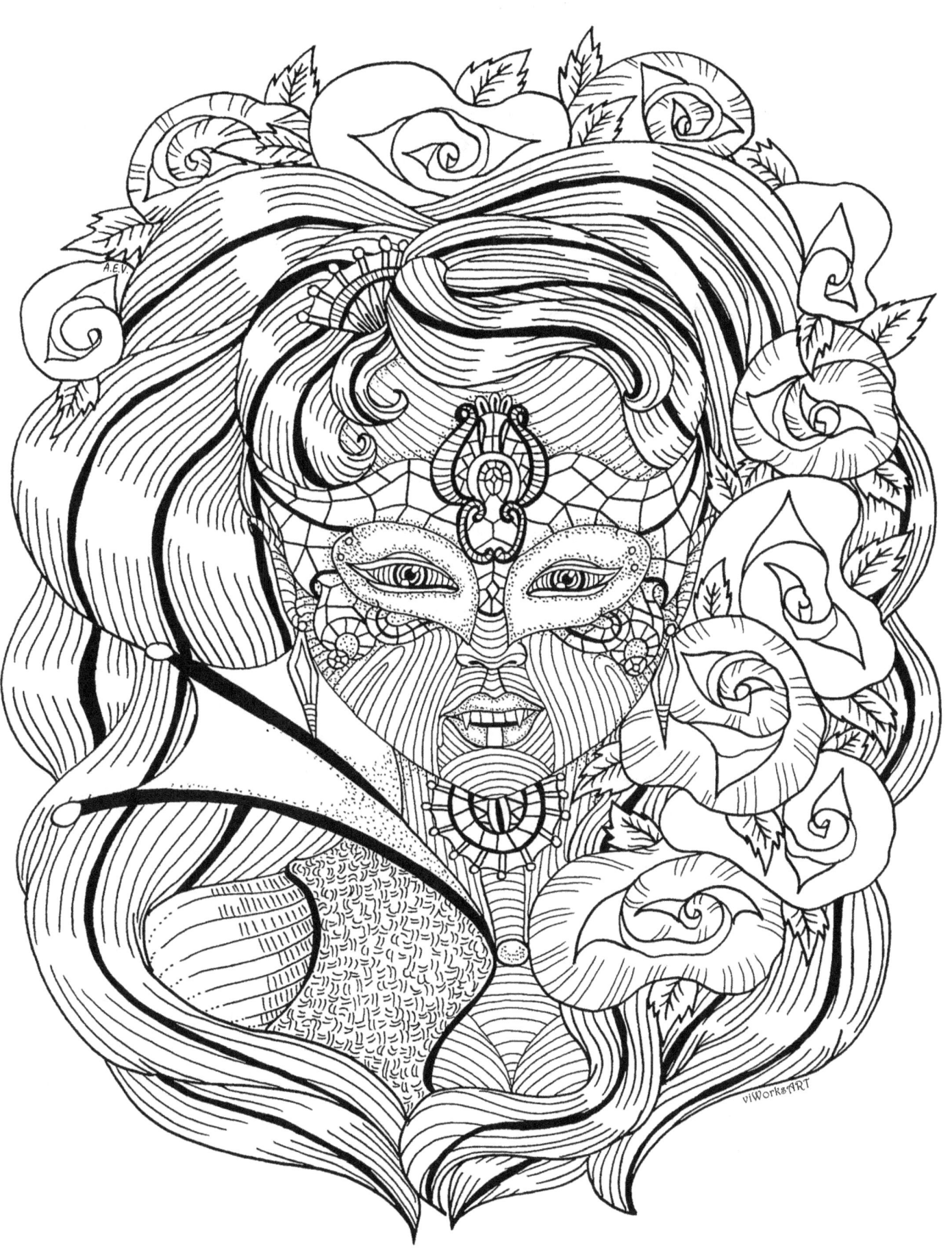

Contributing Artist
Maria Wedeæl
Denmark

Facebook : AMVWART

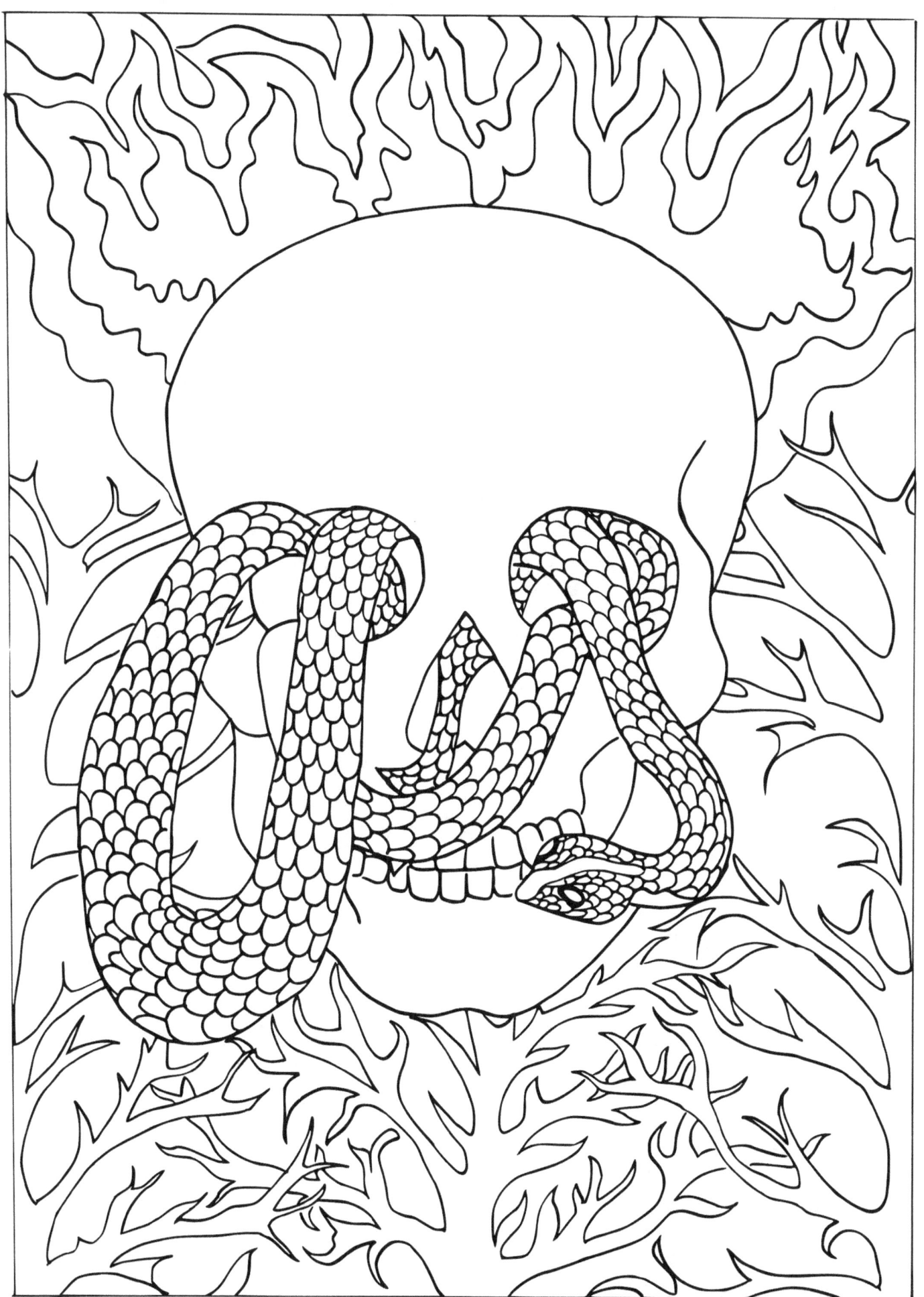

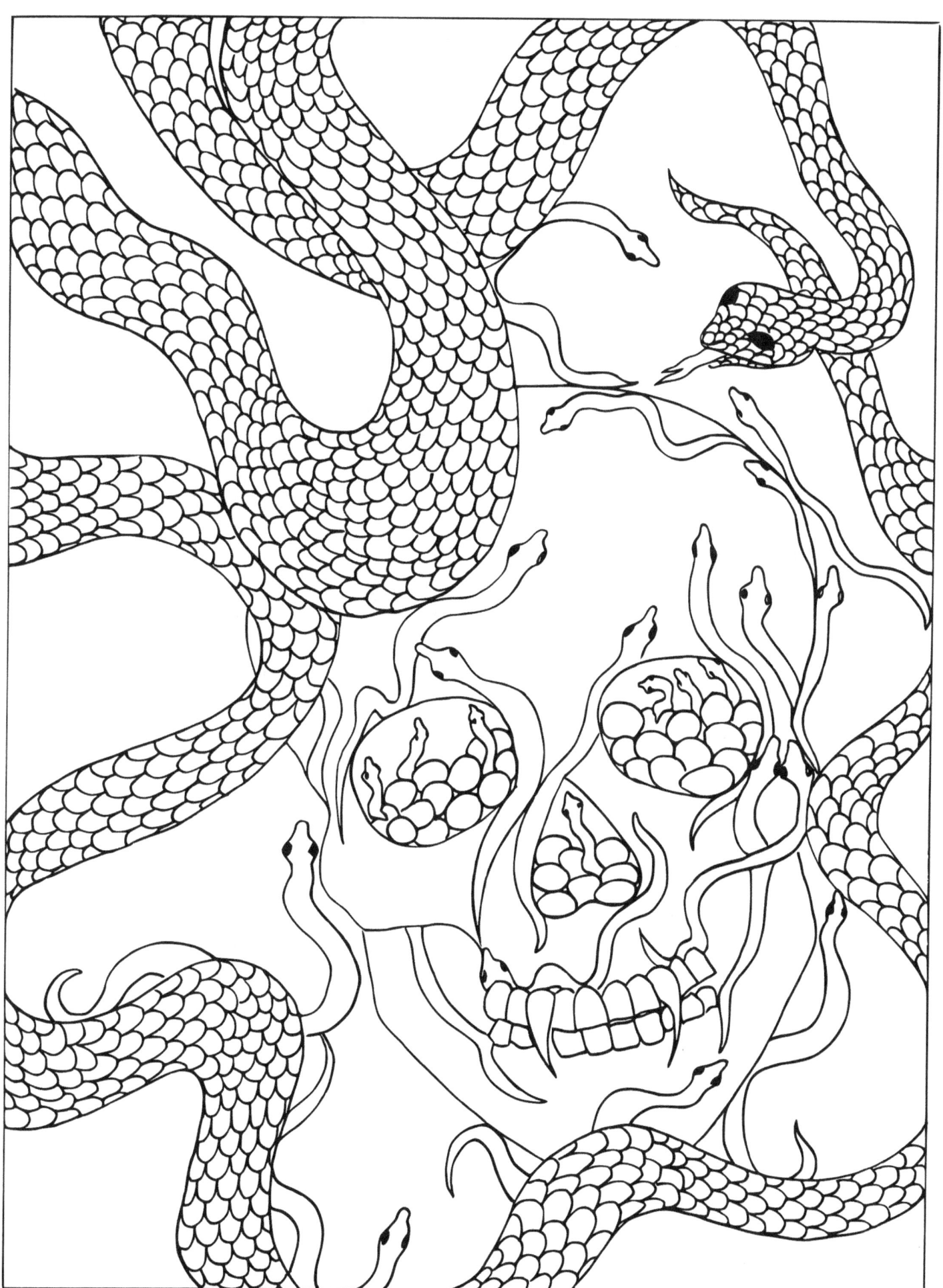

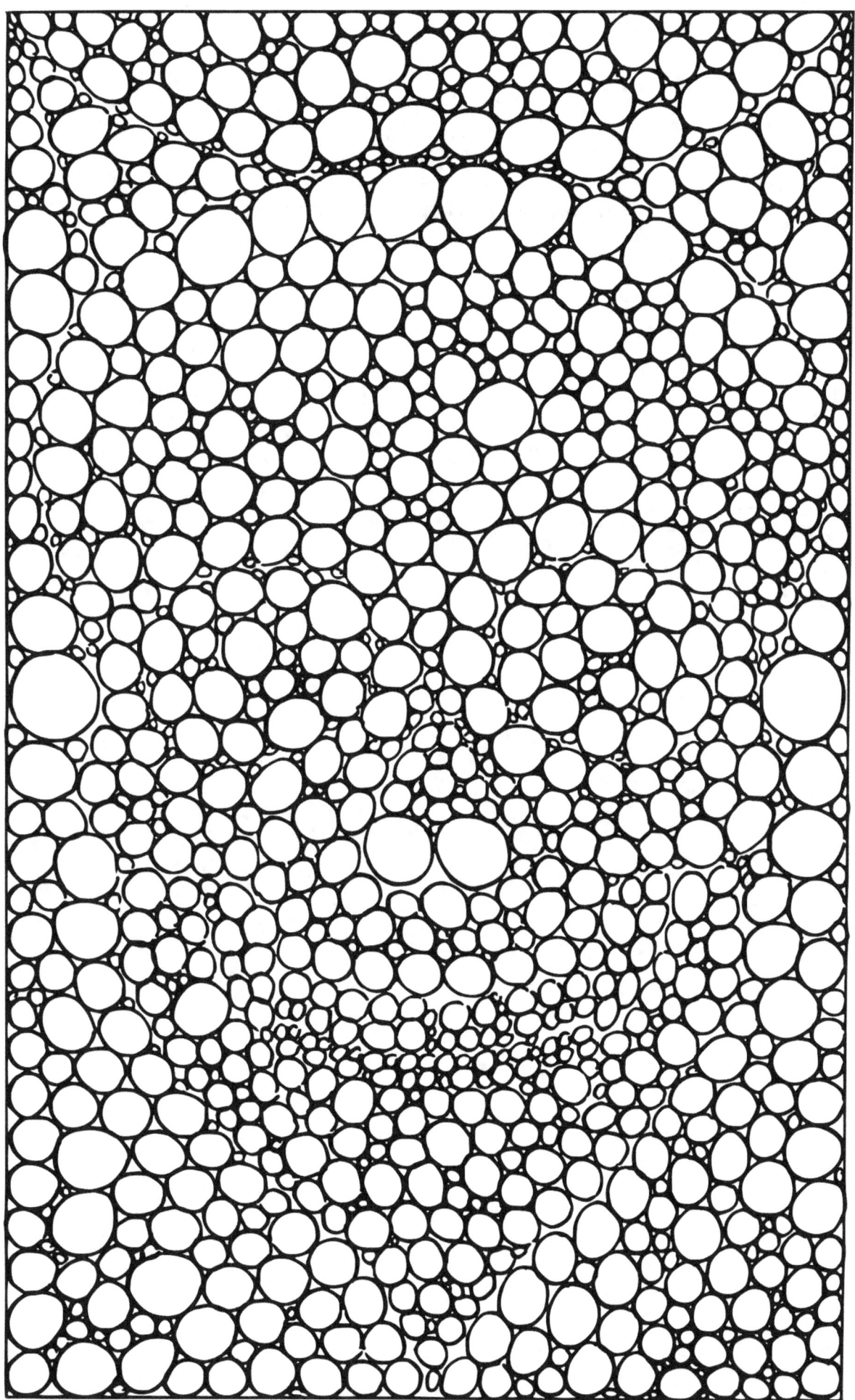

Contributing Artist
Carol Mayer
Canada

www.etsy.com/shop/canadianartbeat

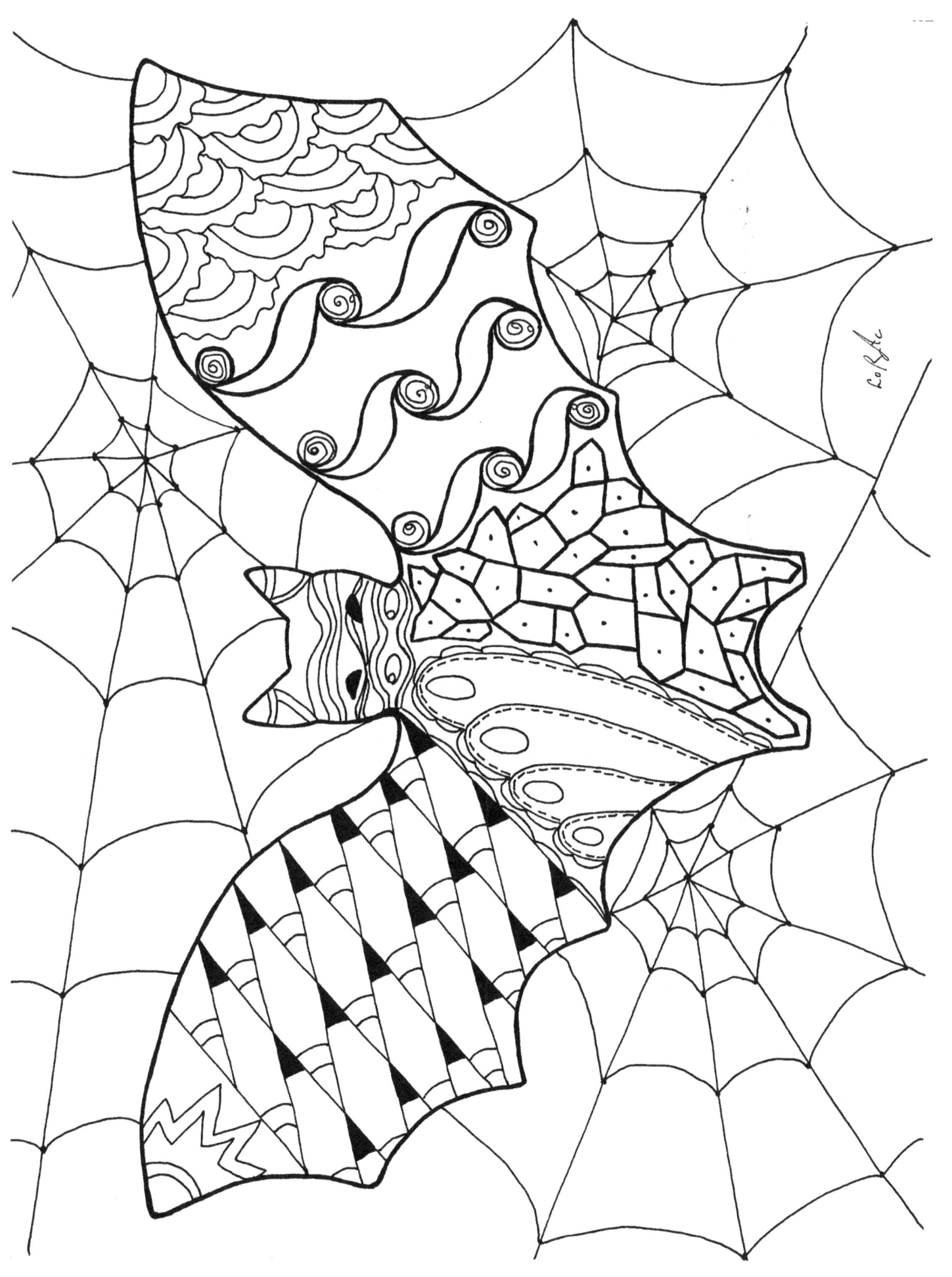

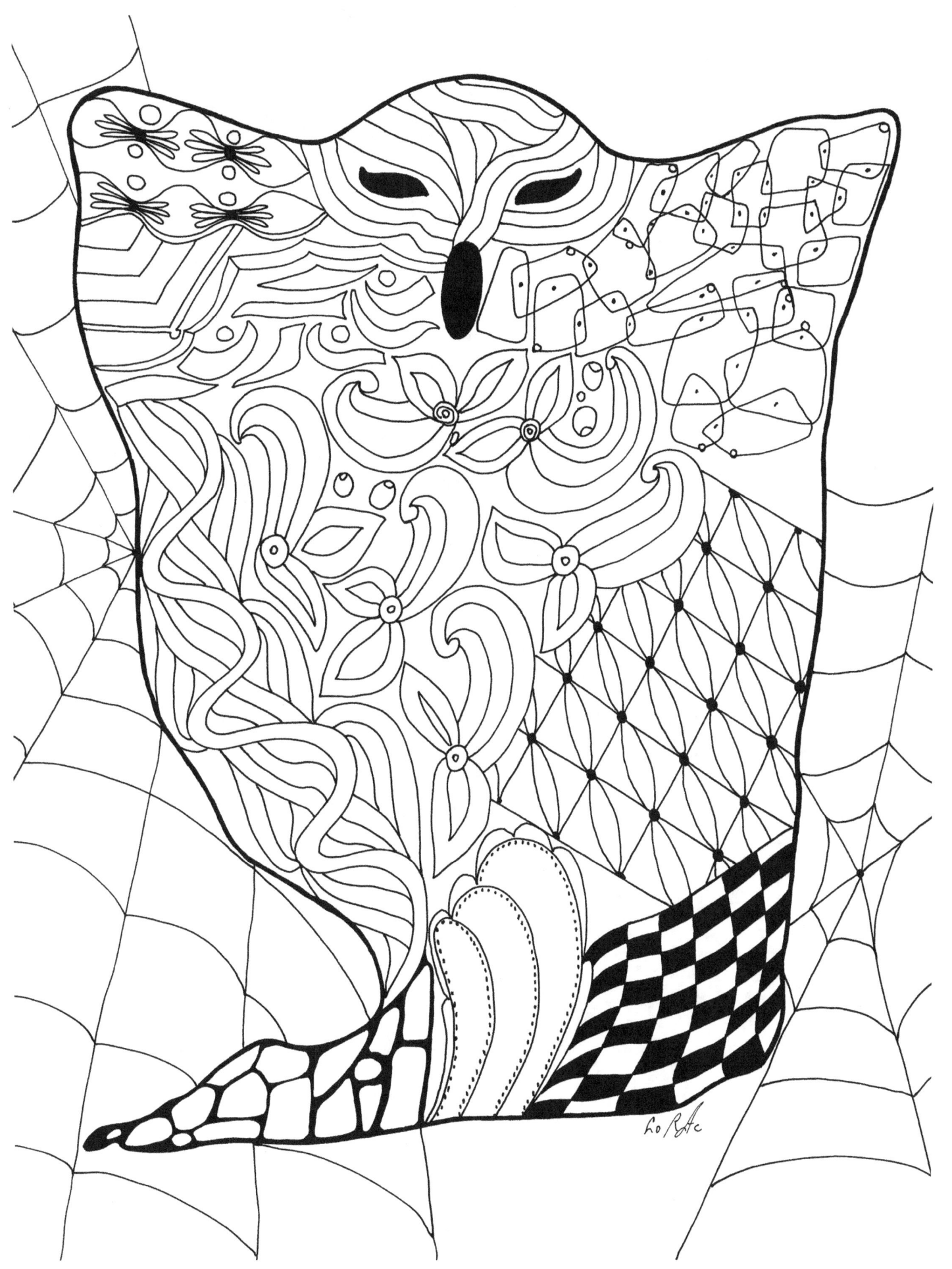

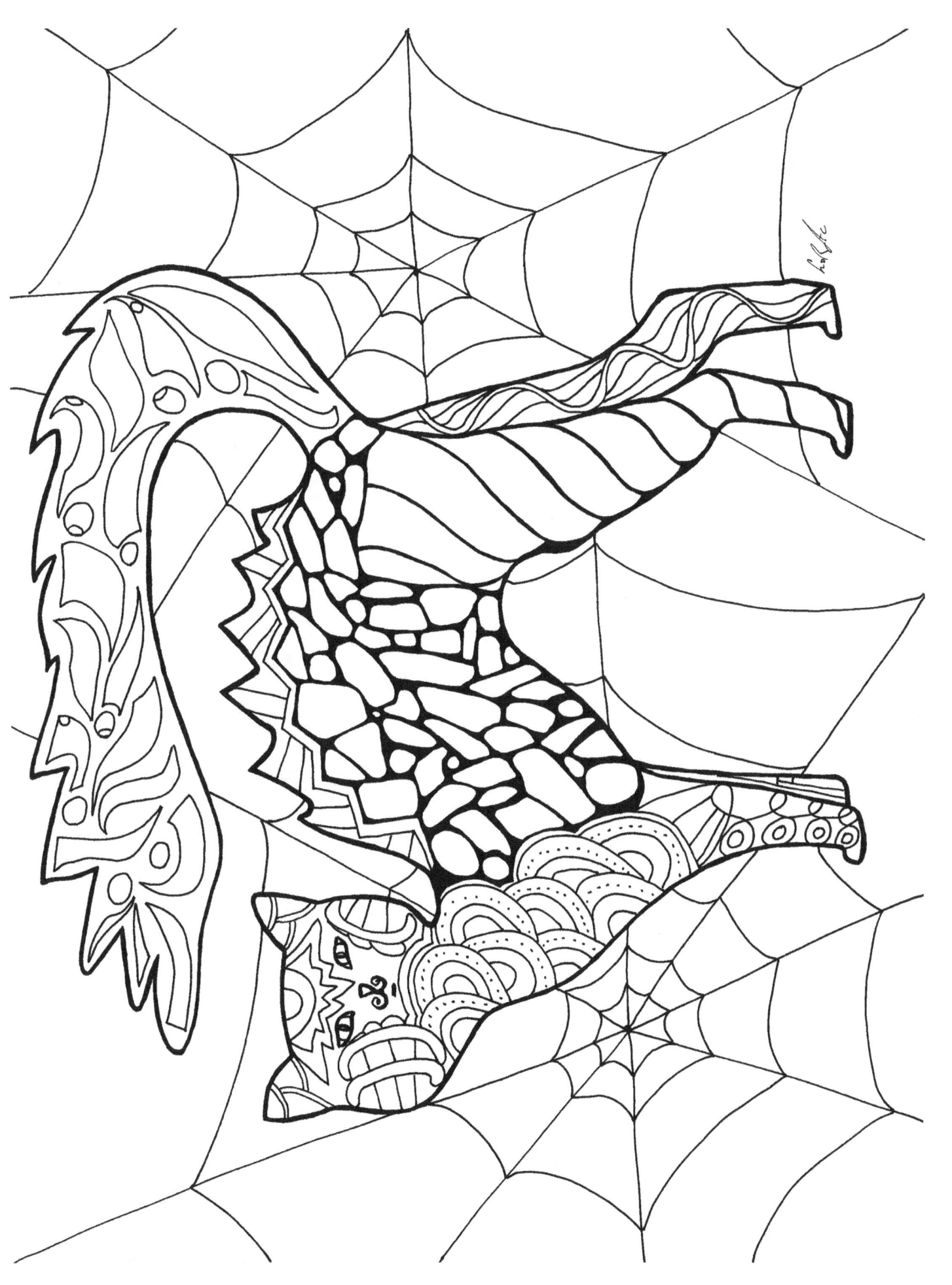

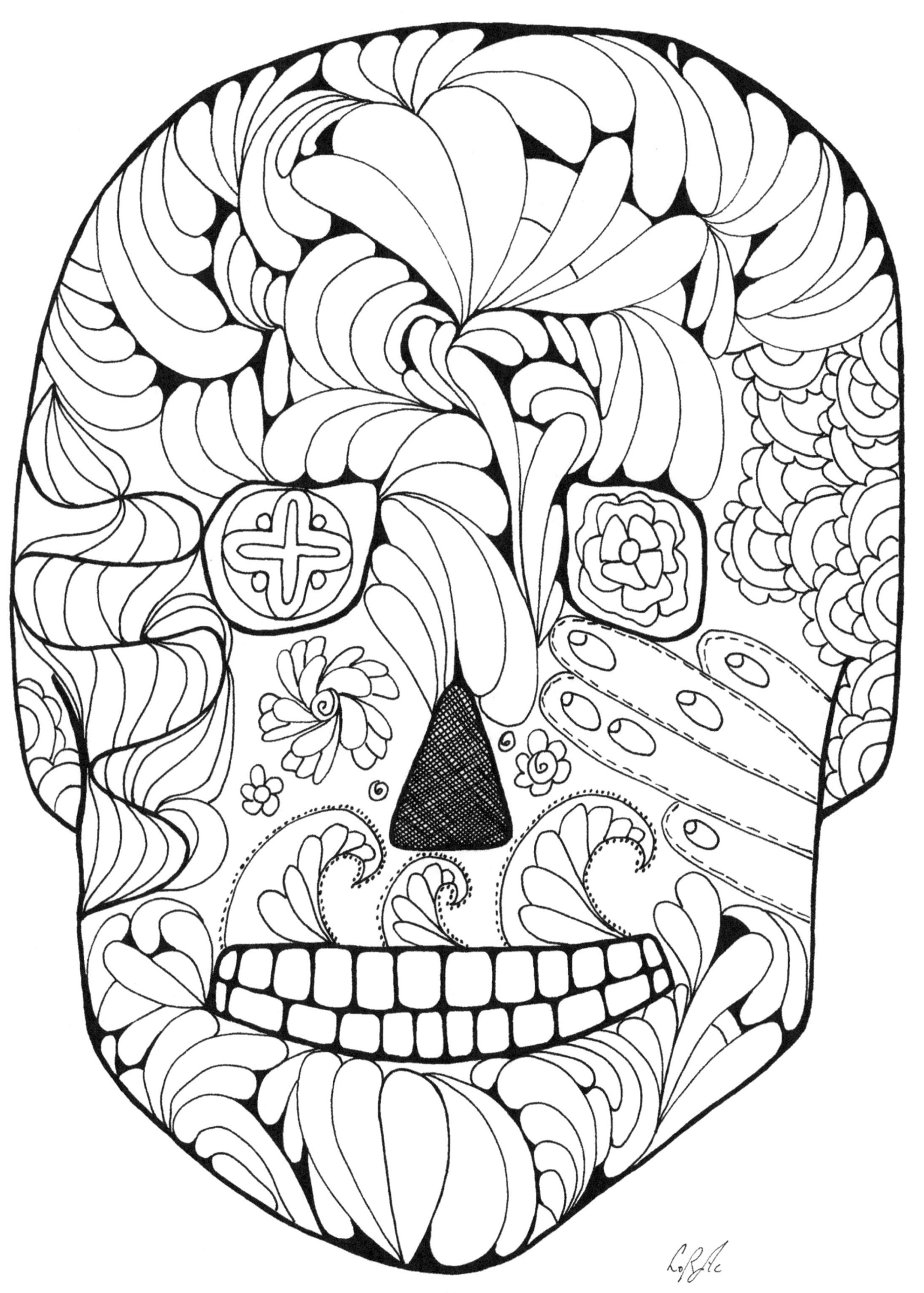

Contributing Artist
Charlotte Fischer
USA

www.scottsmarketplace.com/store/therainbowweb

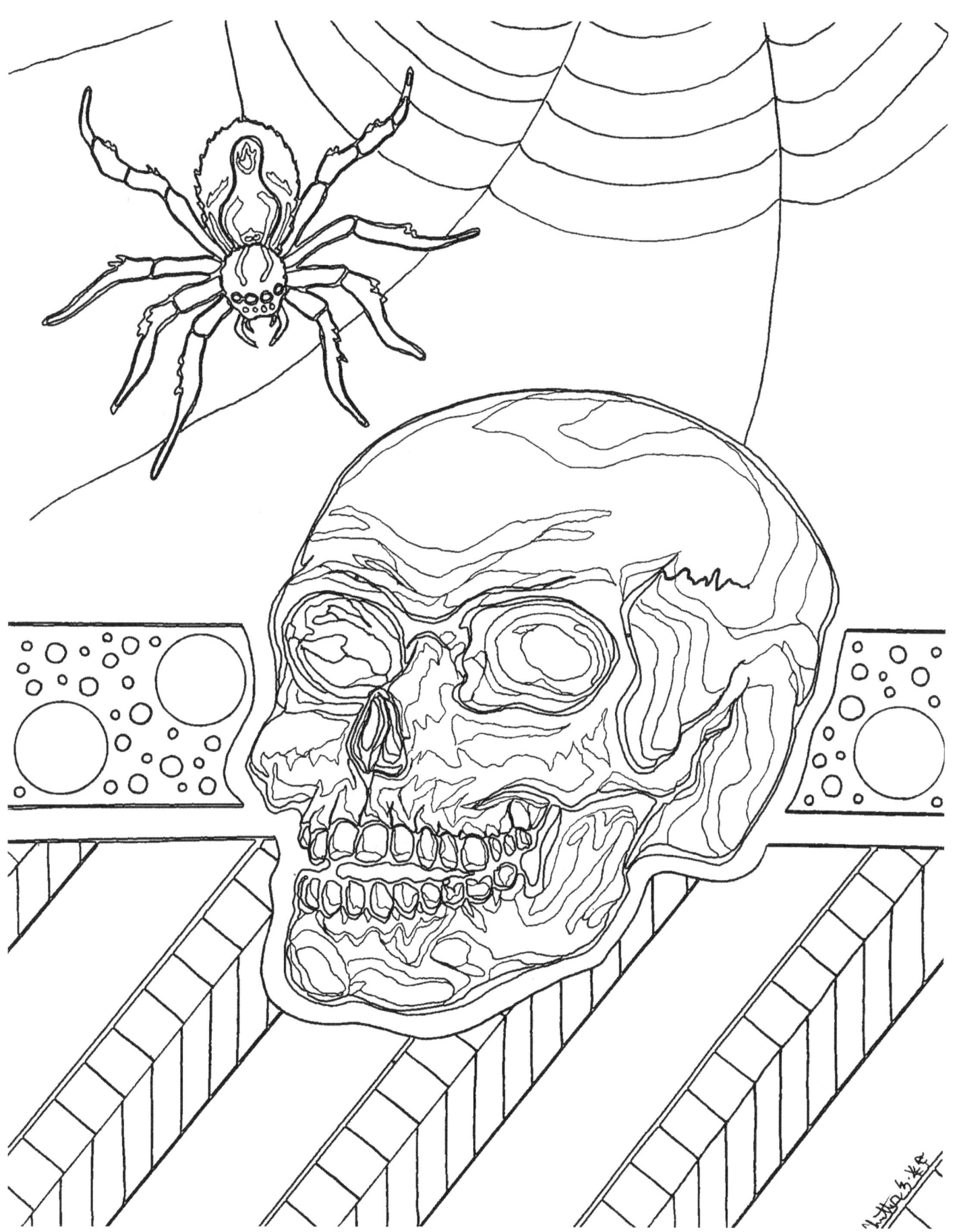

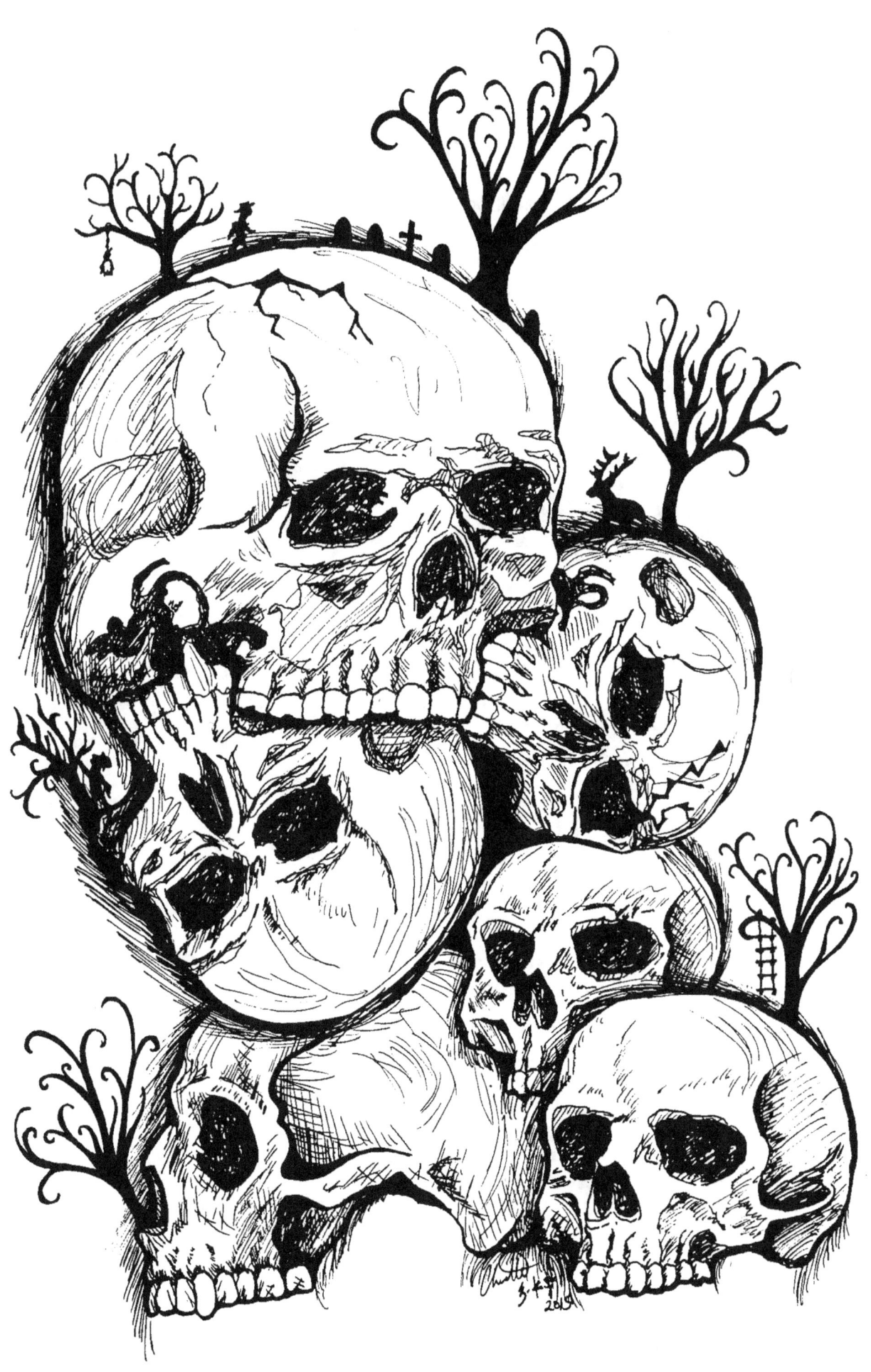

Contributing Artist
Jenny Wei
Taiwan

Facebook : zentangle fun

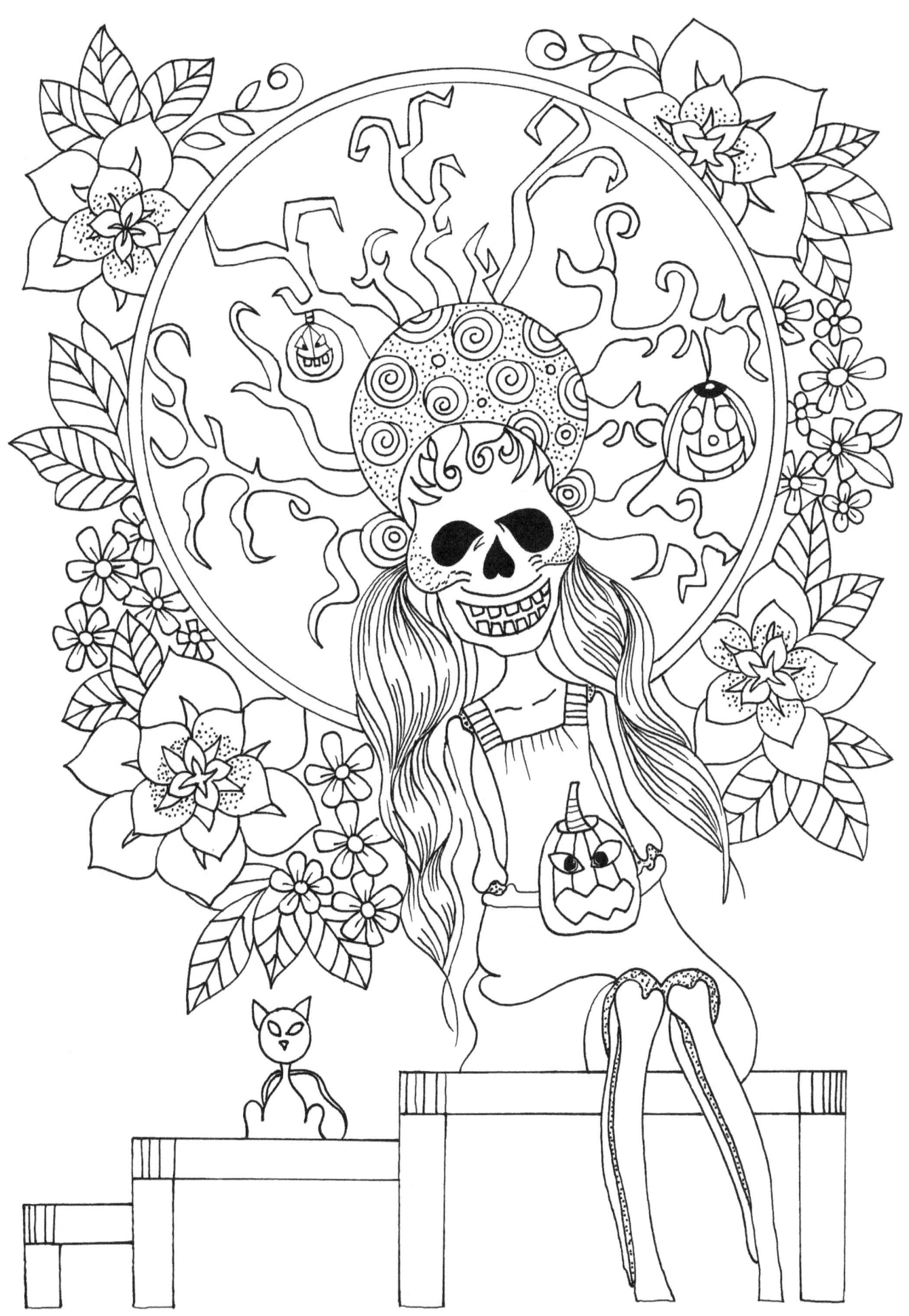

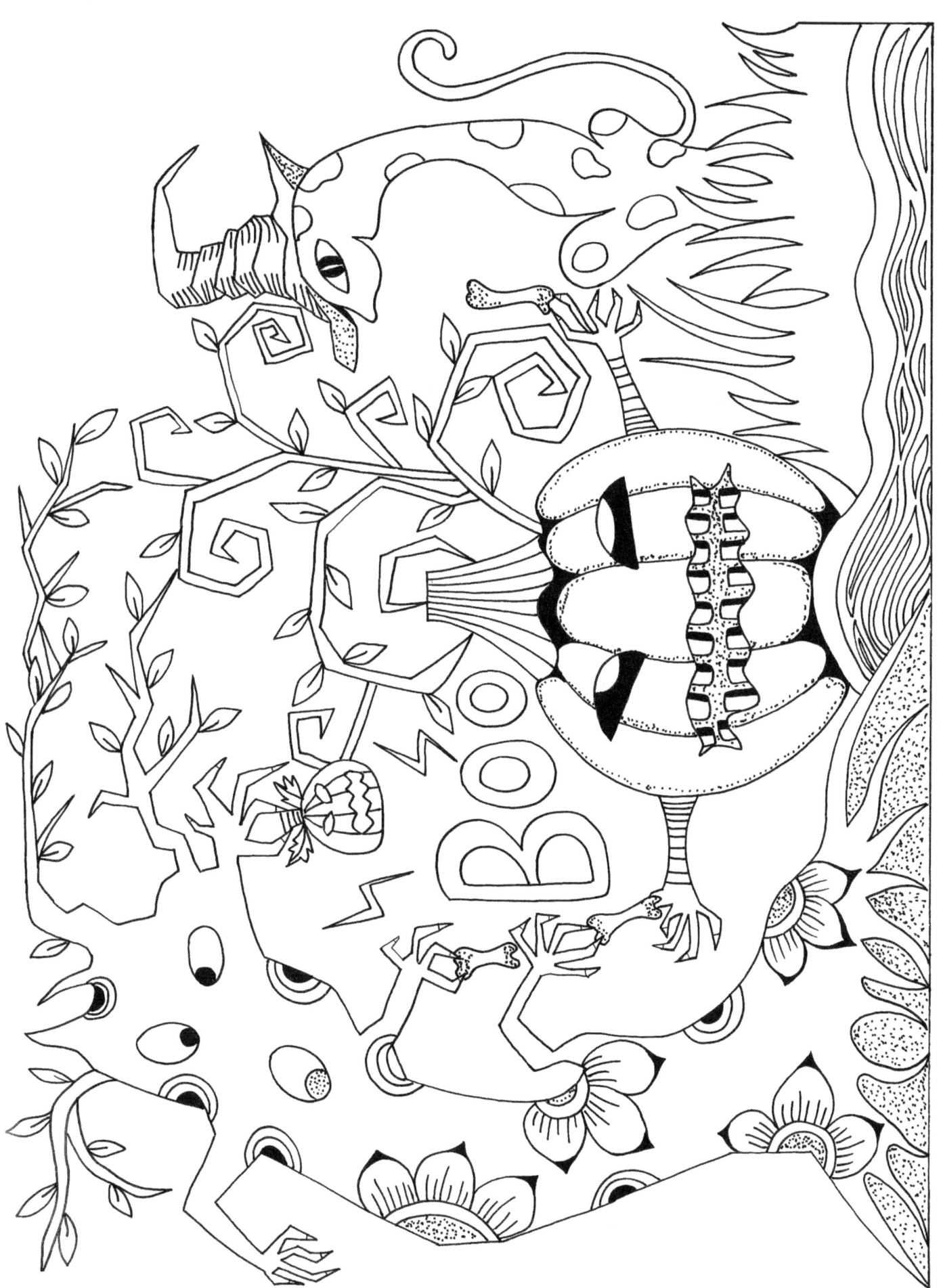

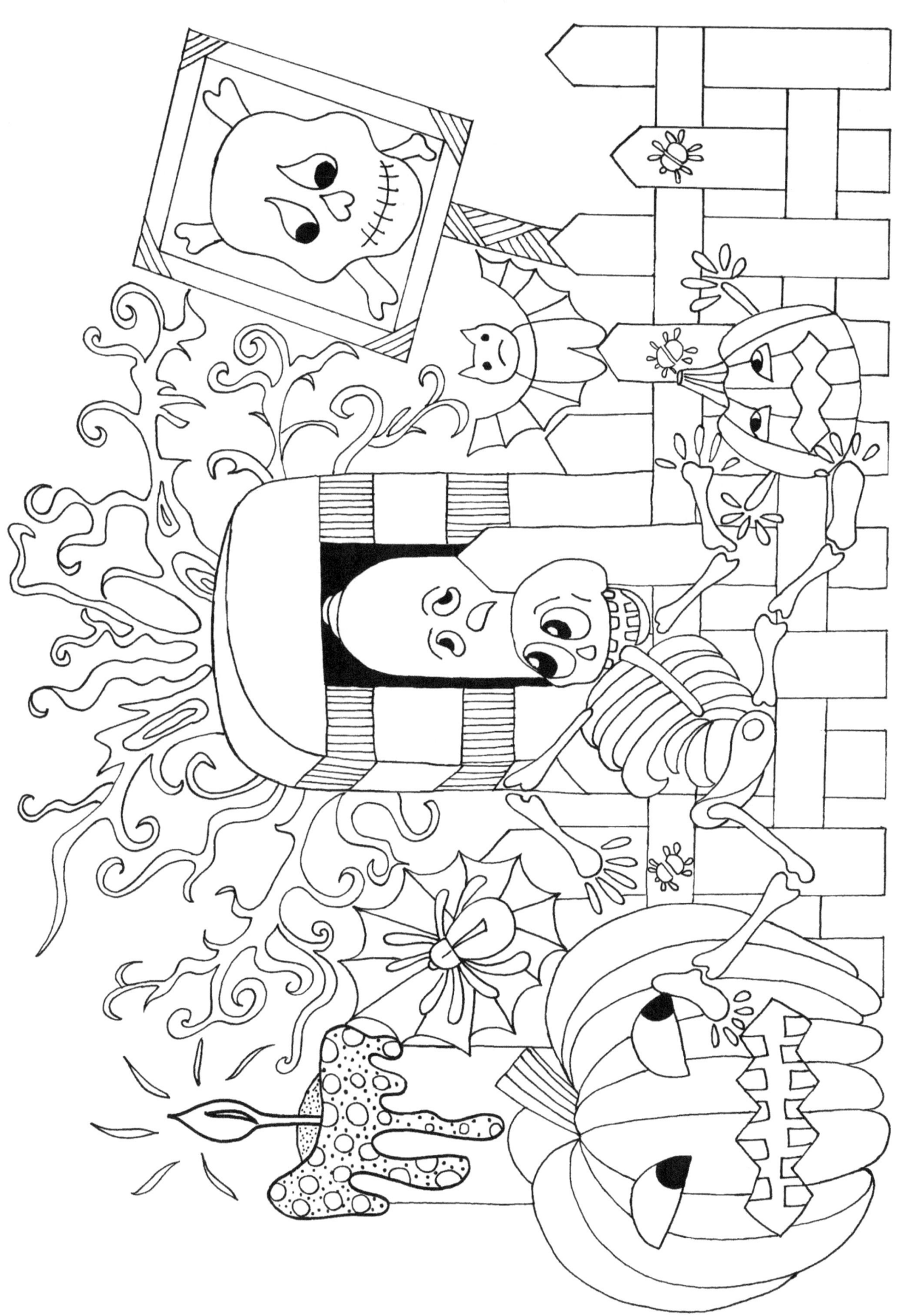

Contributing Artist
Jodi Ho
Taiwan

Facebook : Dream jodi's dream

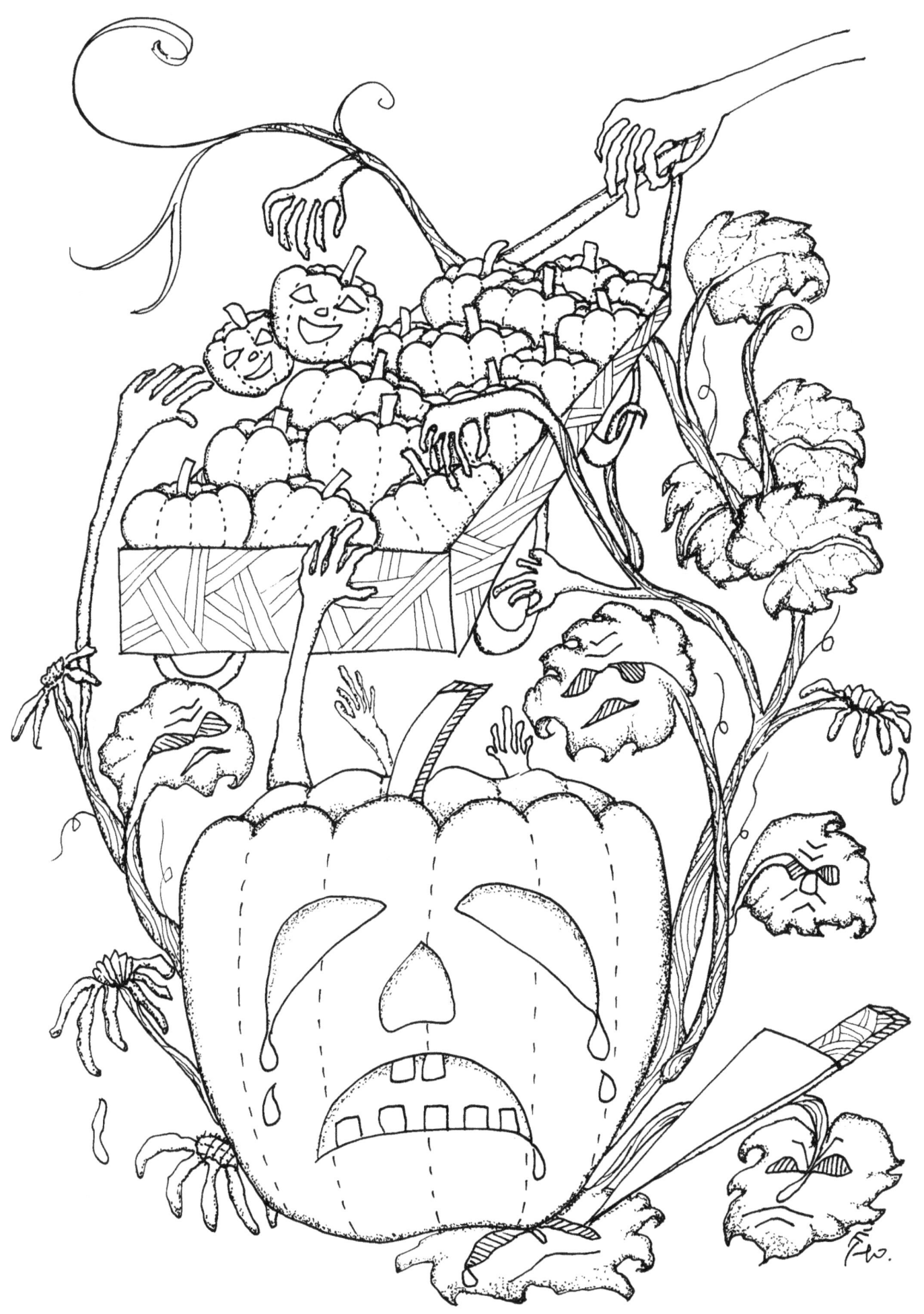

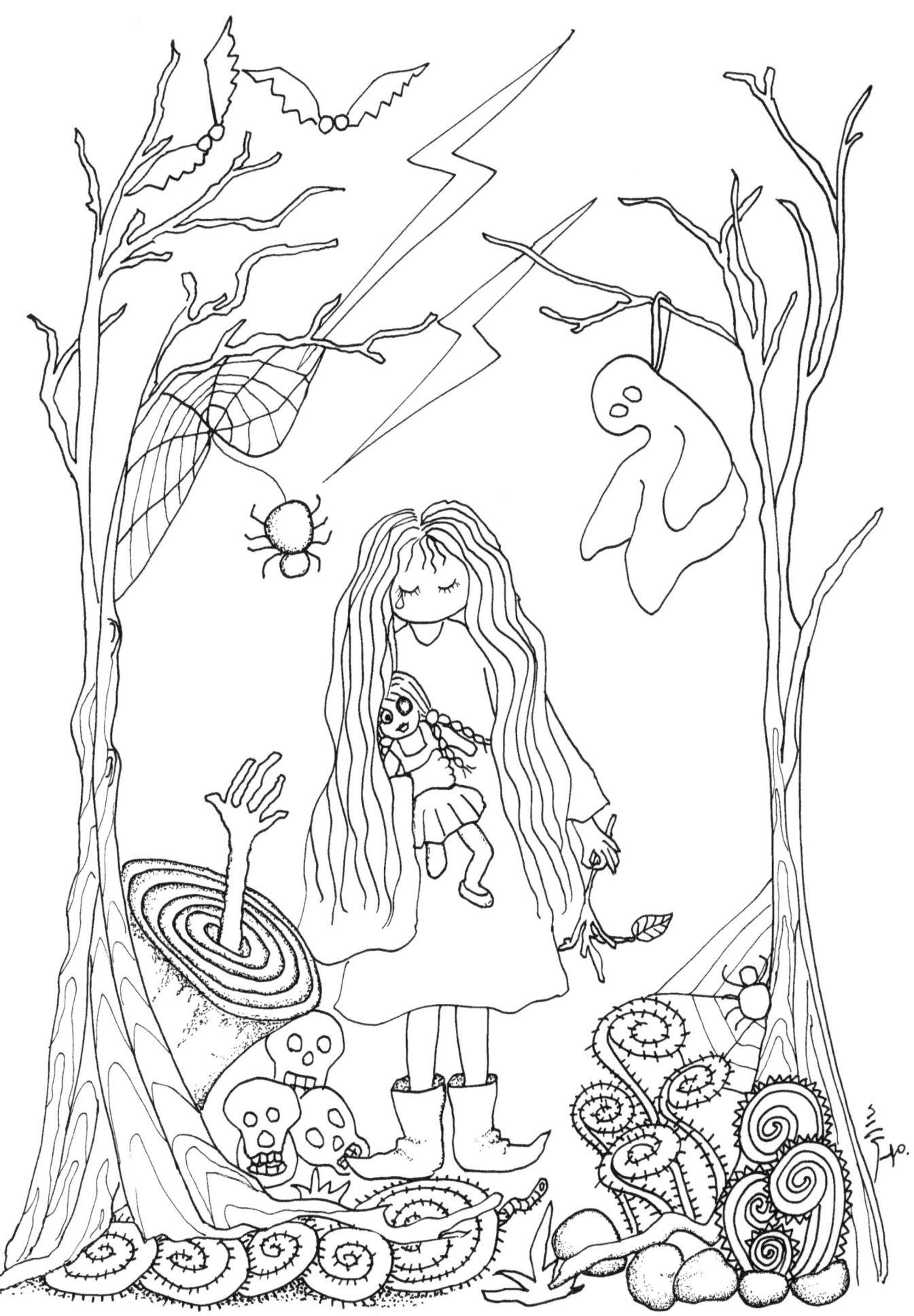

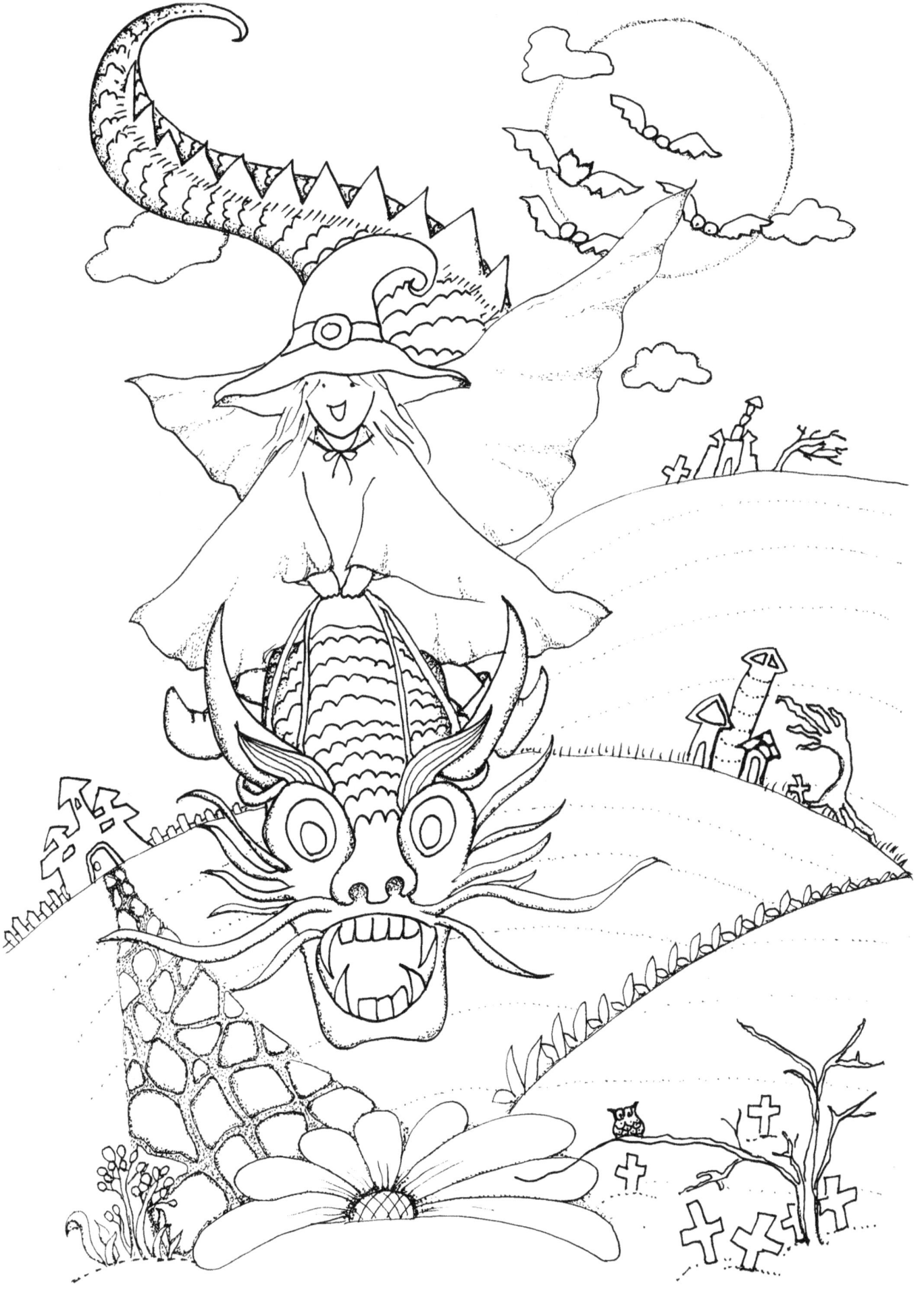

Contributing Artist
Lilan Chen
Taiwan

Facebook : lilanchen.art

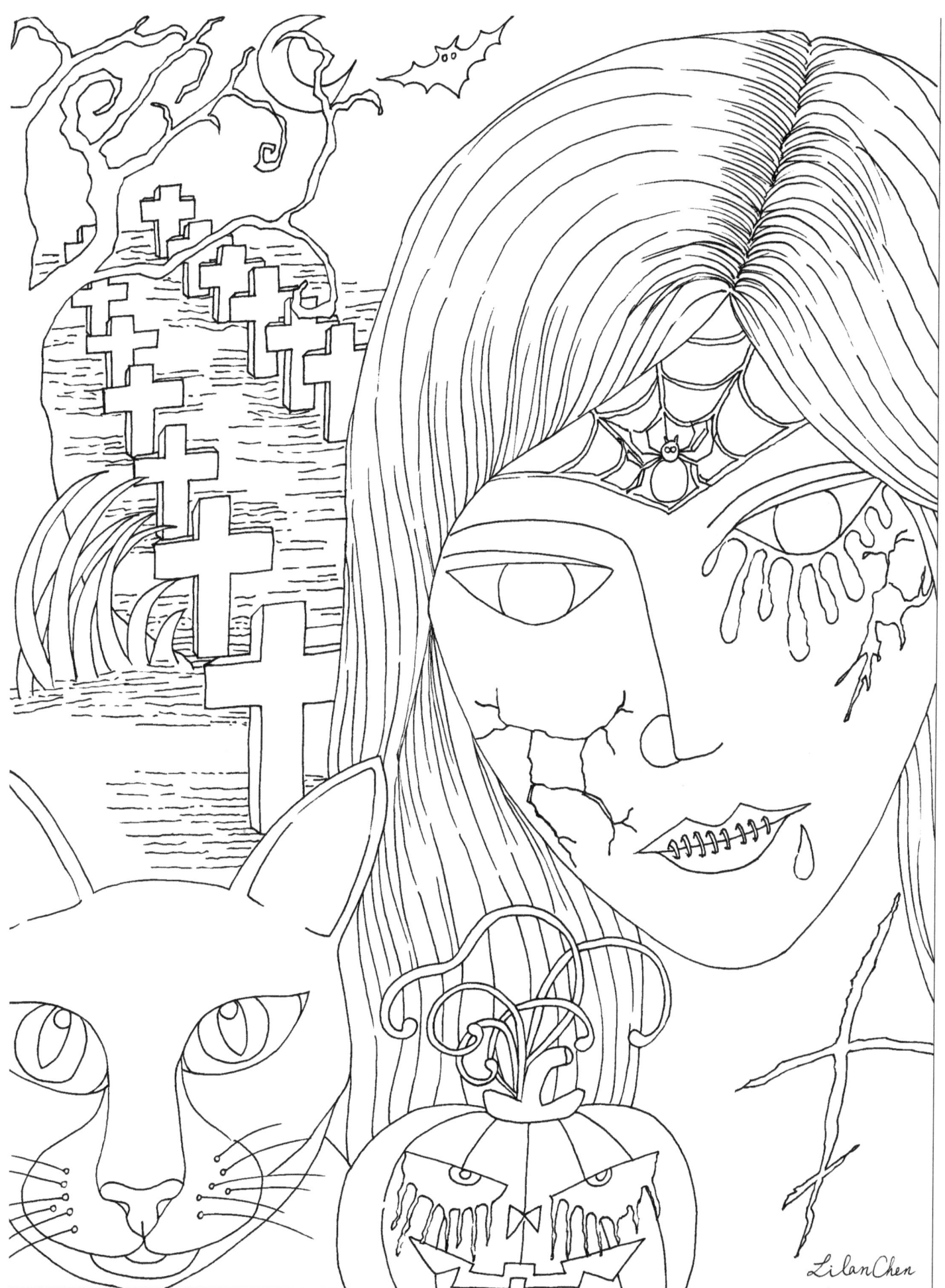

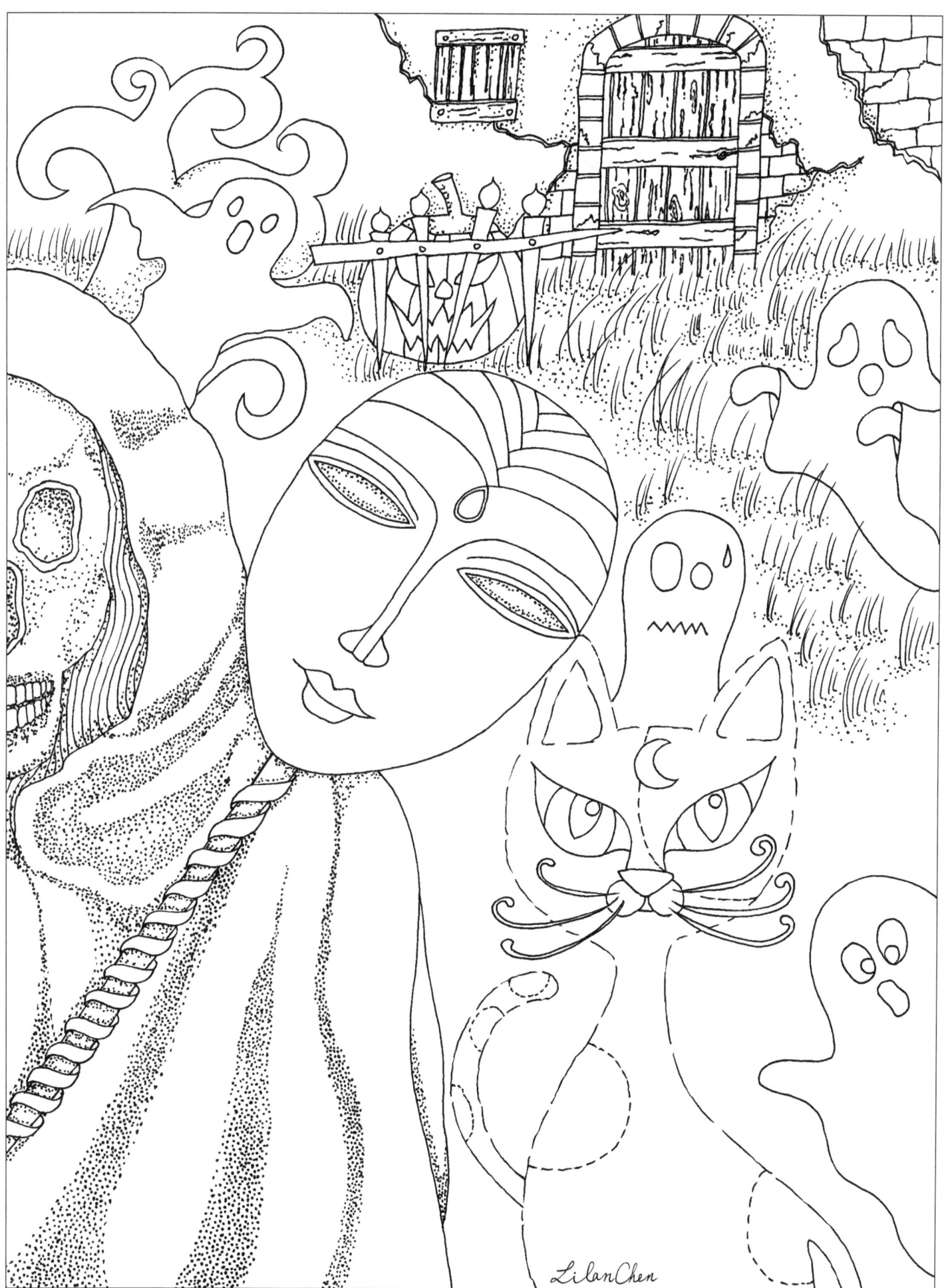

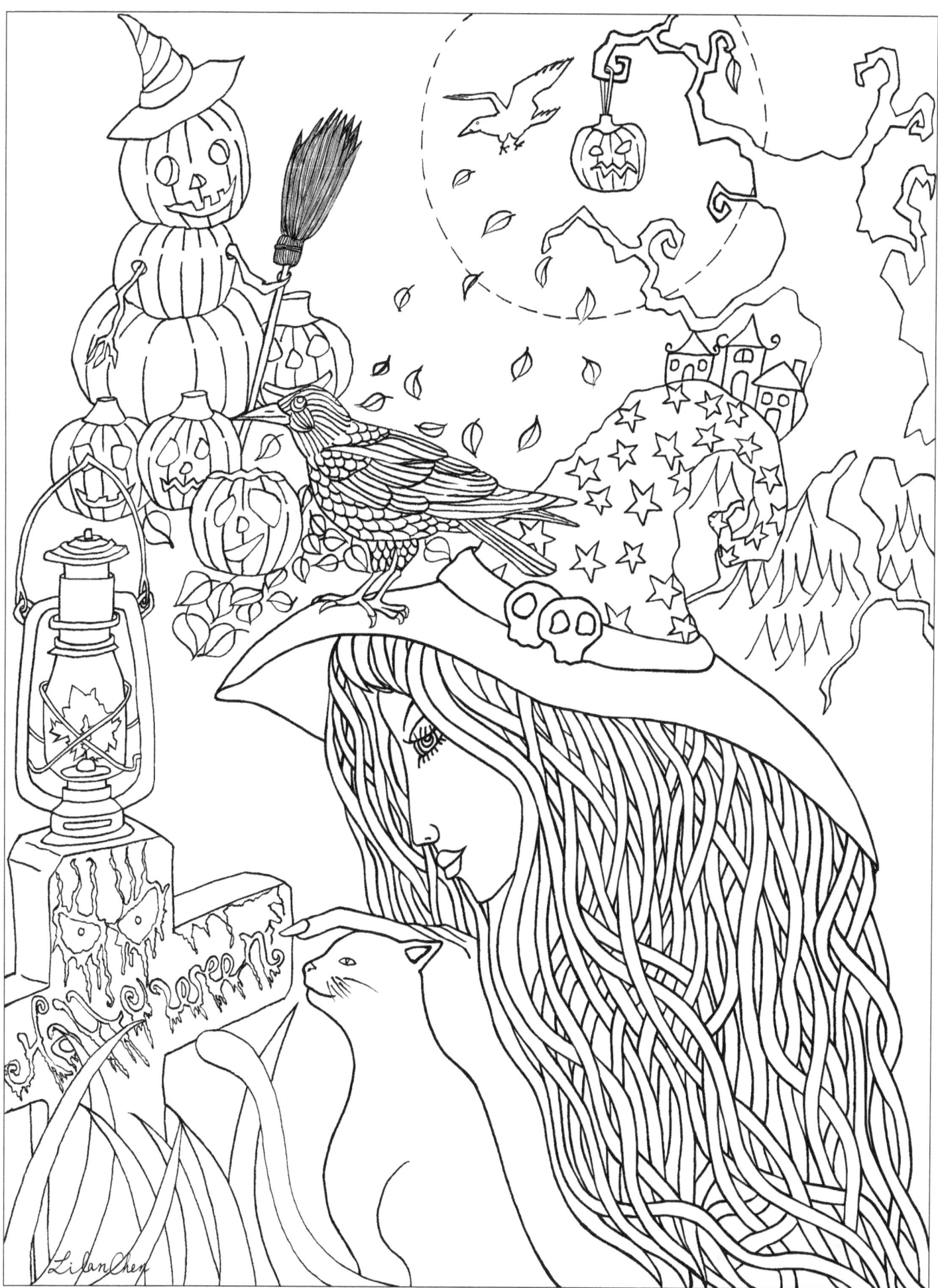

Contributing Artist
Nancy43
Taiwan

Facebook : Pajun Chen

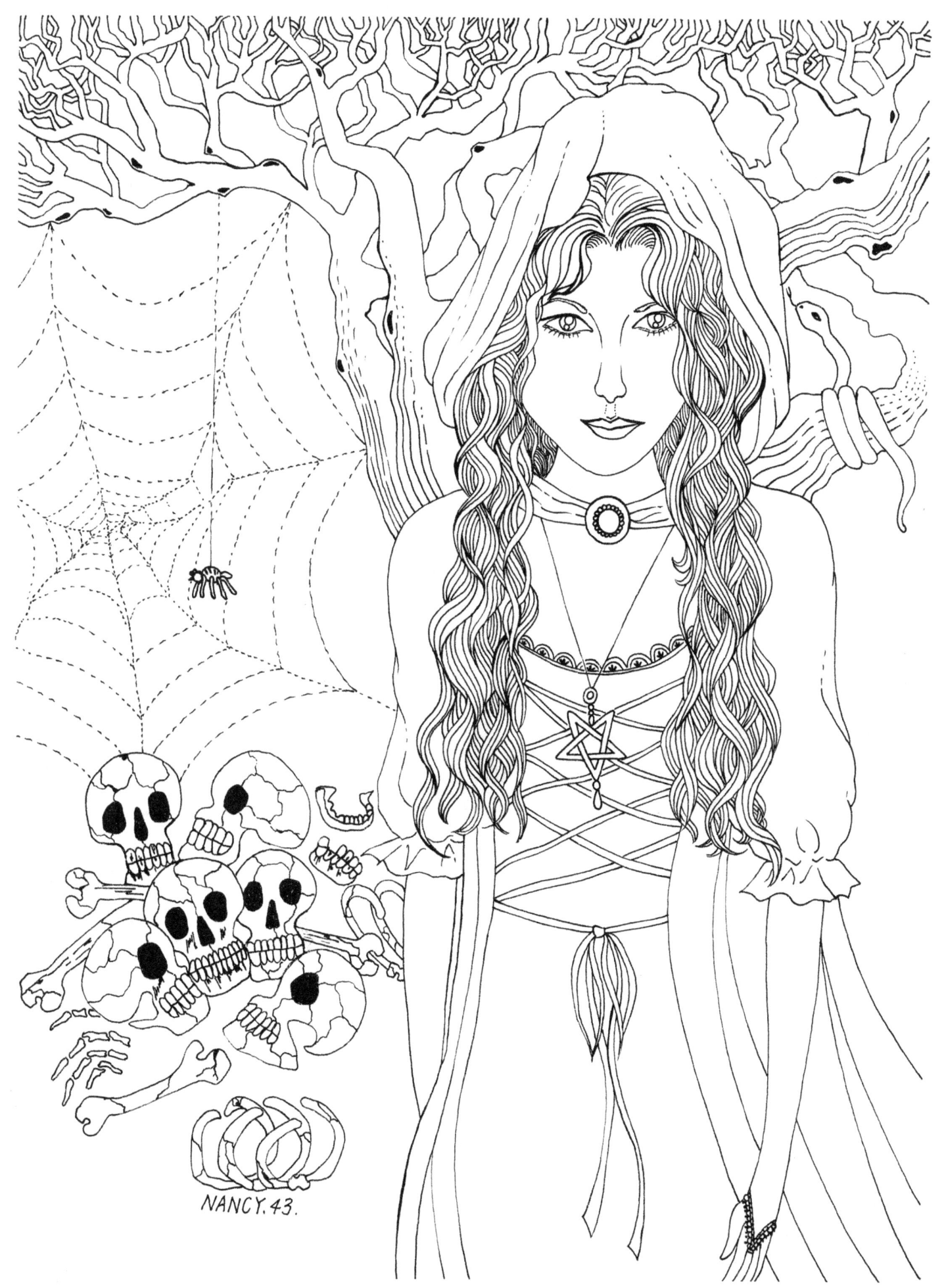

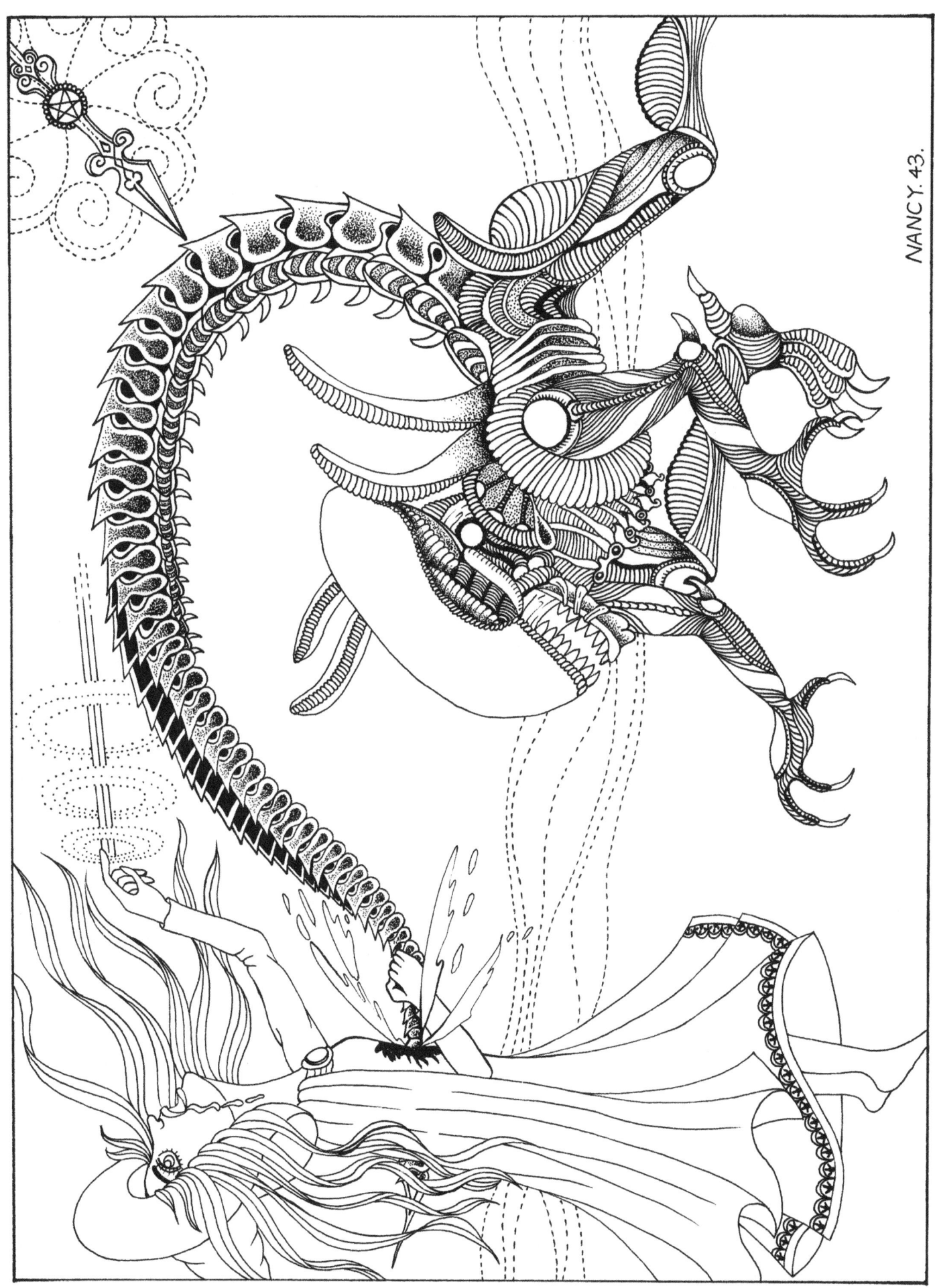

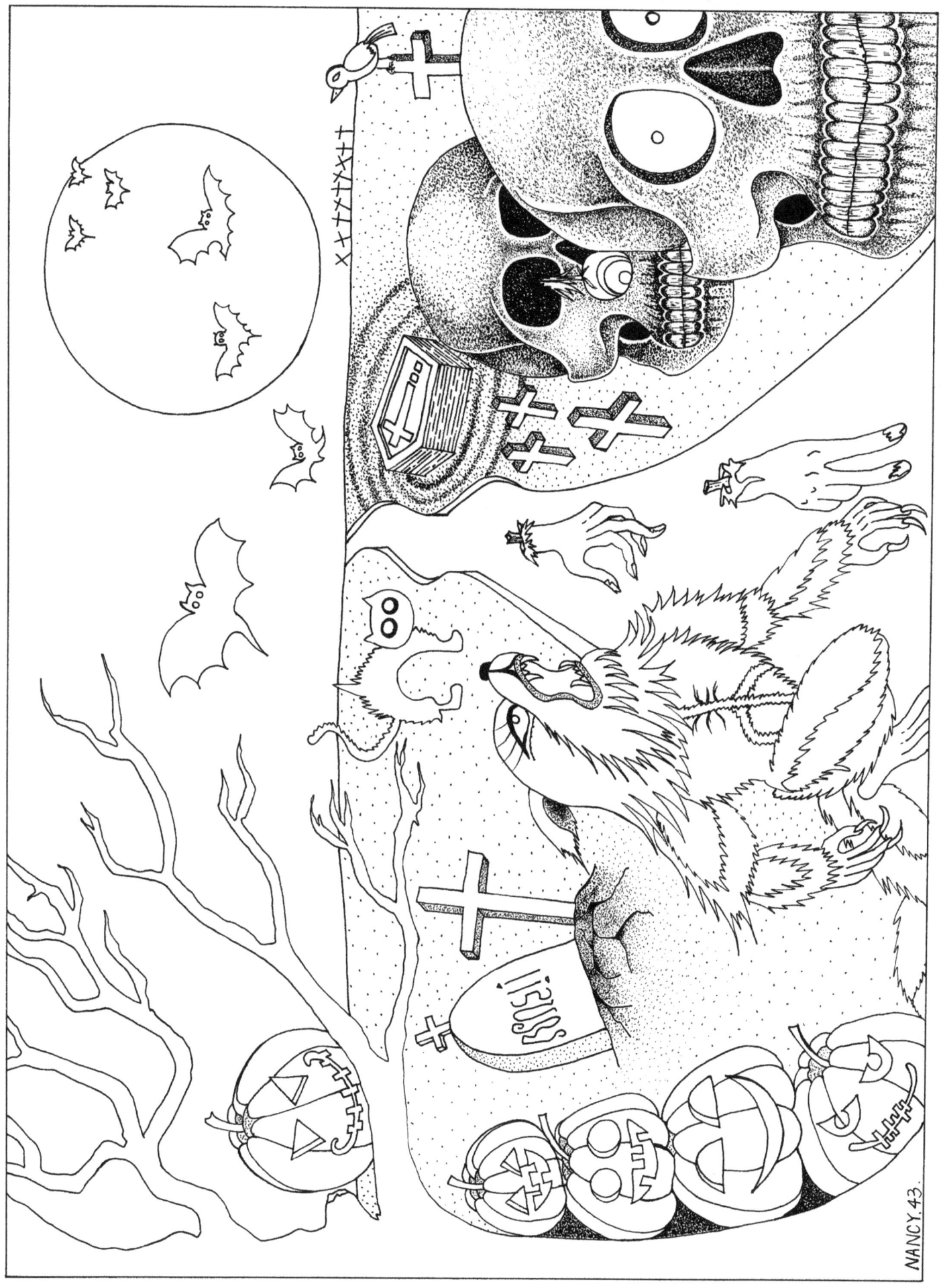

Contributing Artist
Pajun Chen
Taiwan

Facebook : Pajun Chen

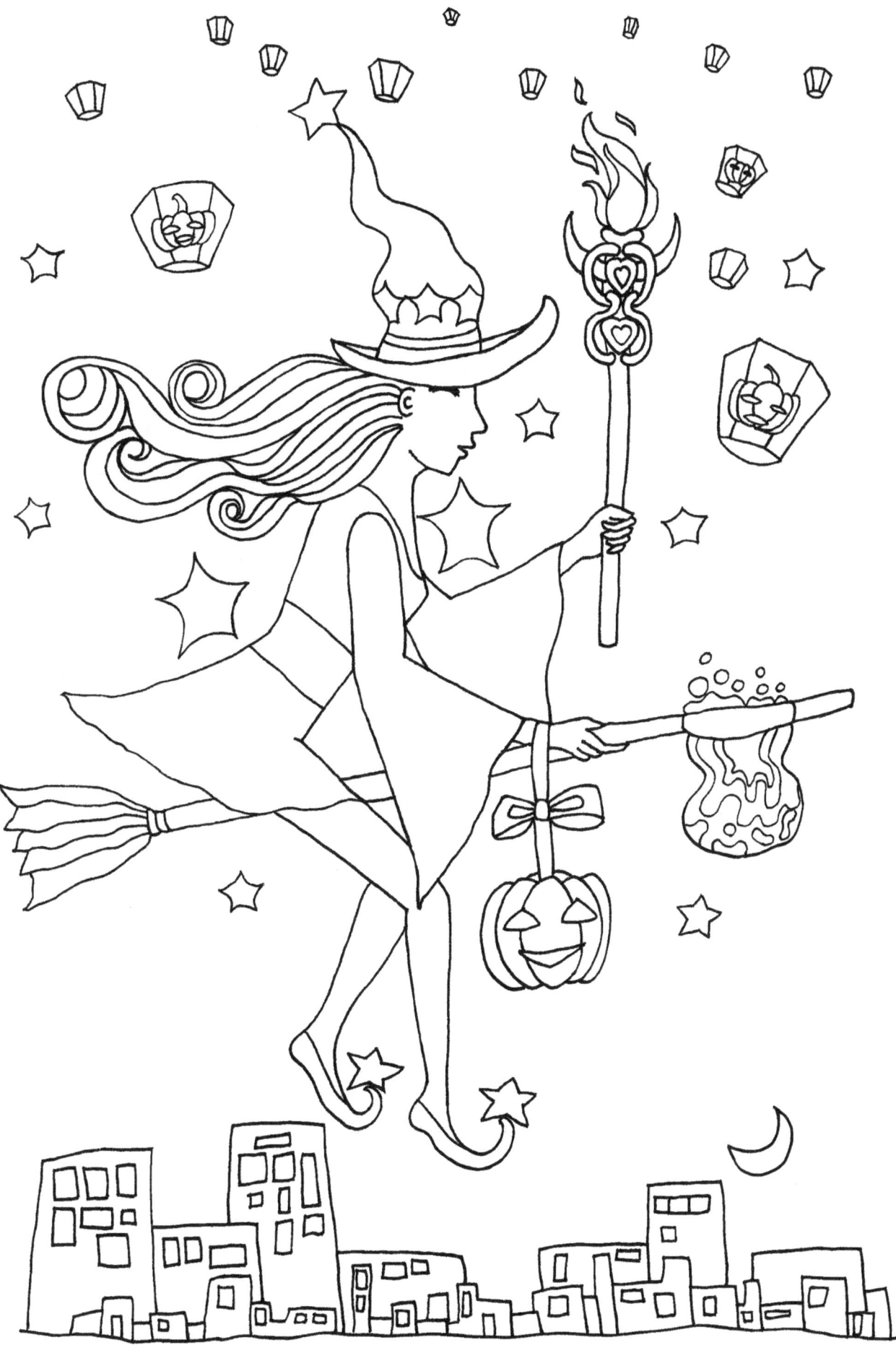

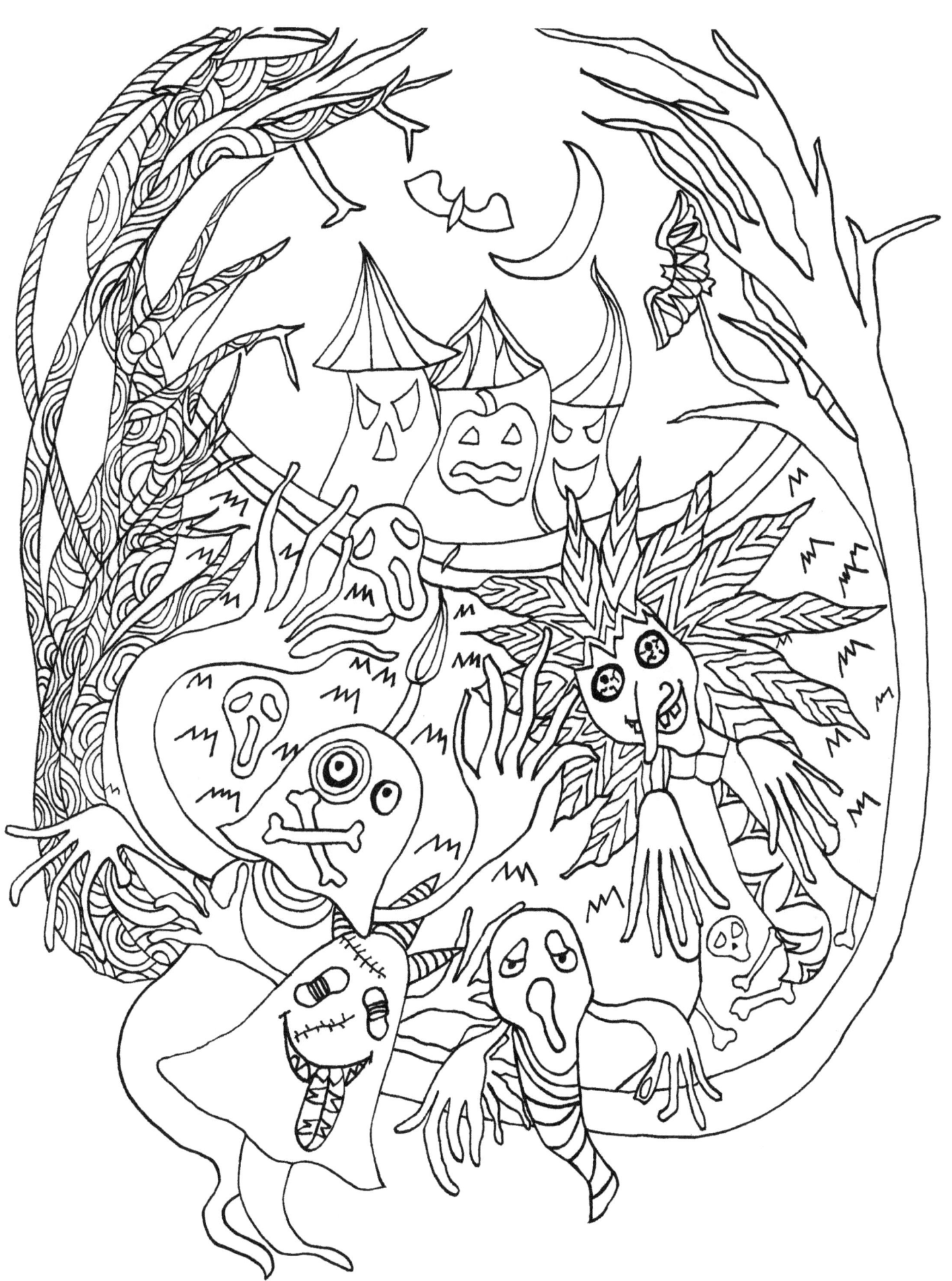

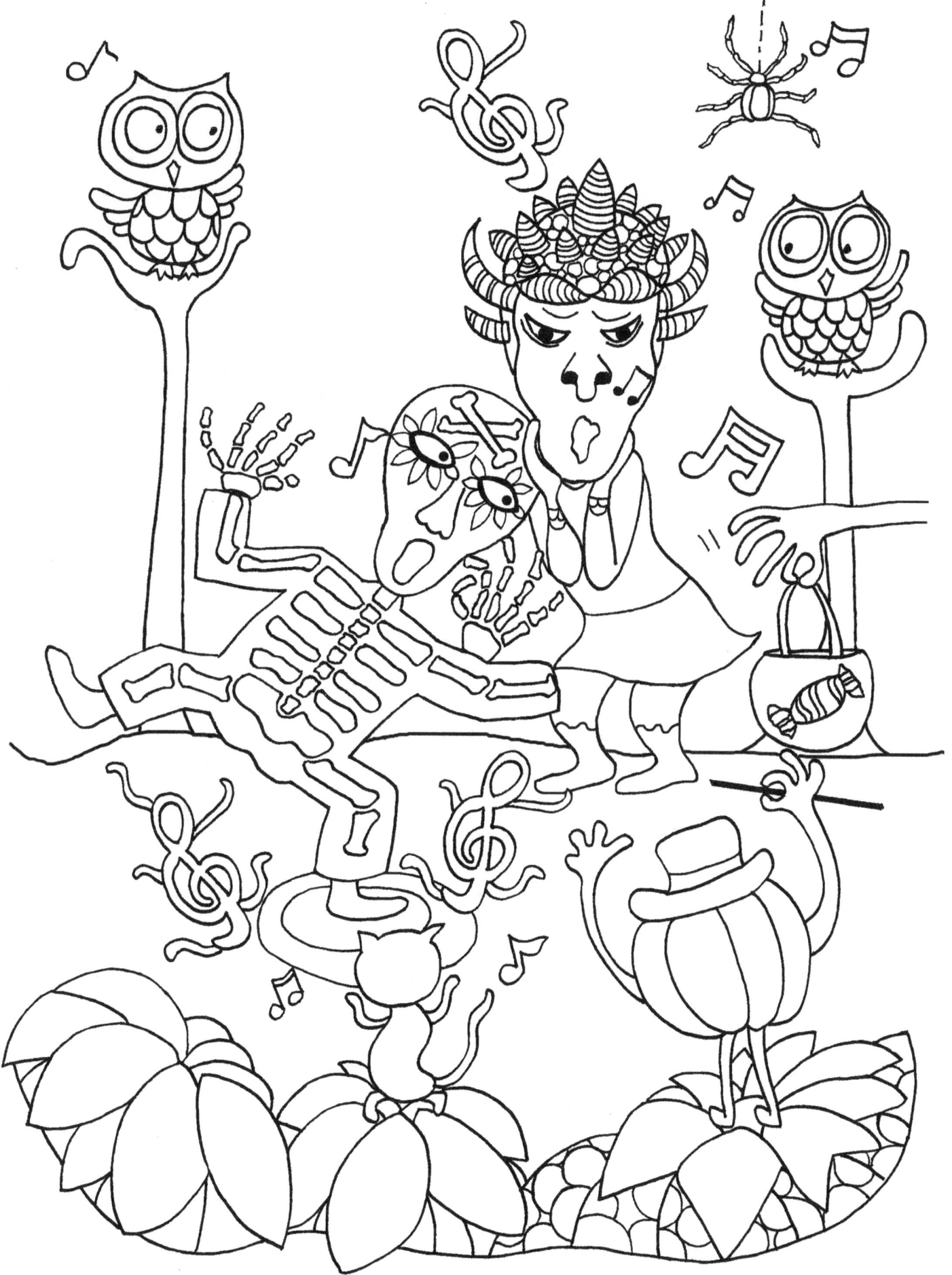

Contributing Artist
Pica Wu
Taiwan

Facebook : Pica's Zentangle Art

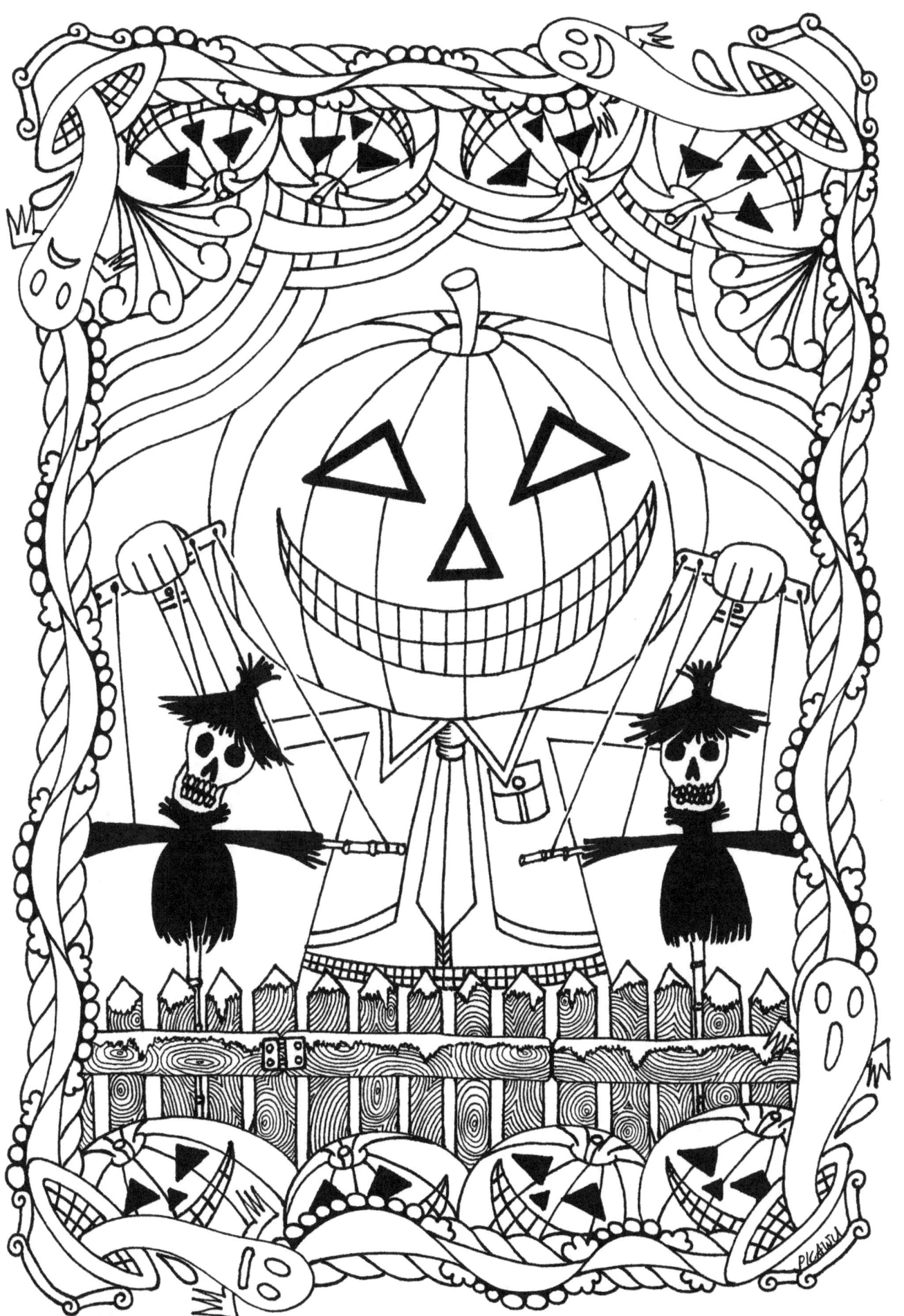

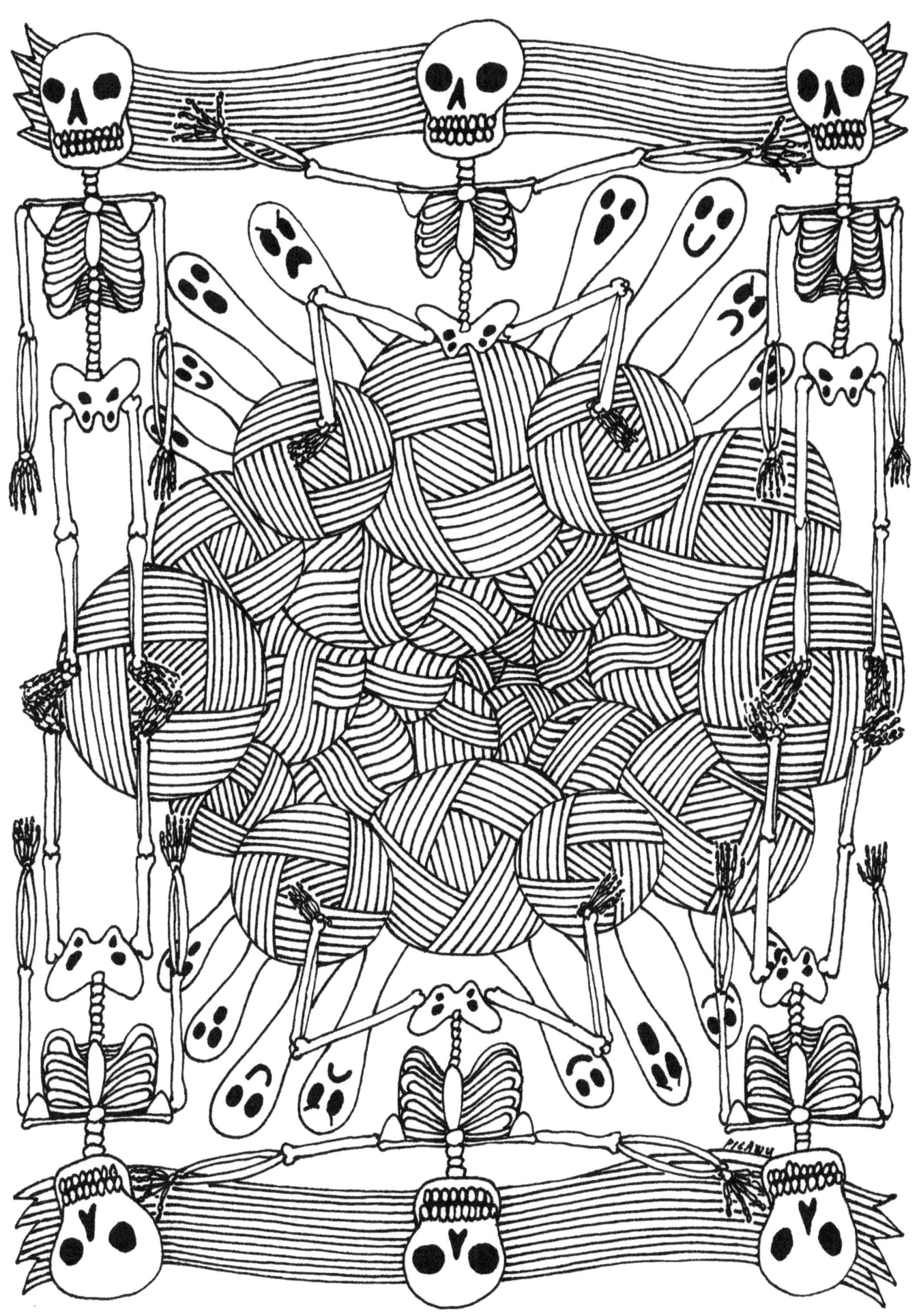

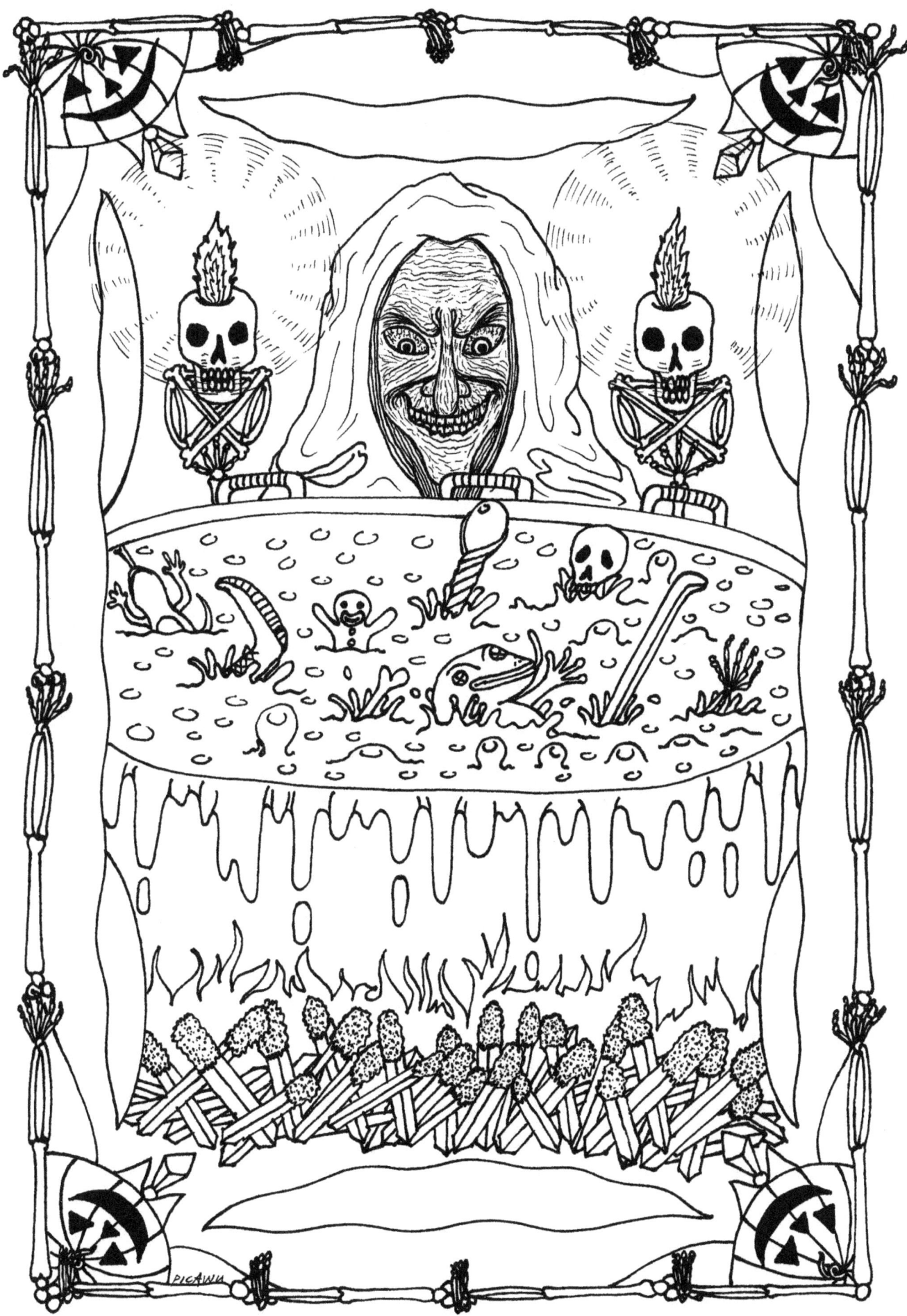

Contributing Artist
Rover Hsiao
Taiwan

Facebook : roverhsiao2015

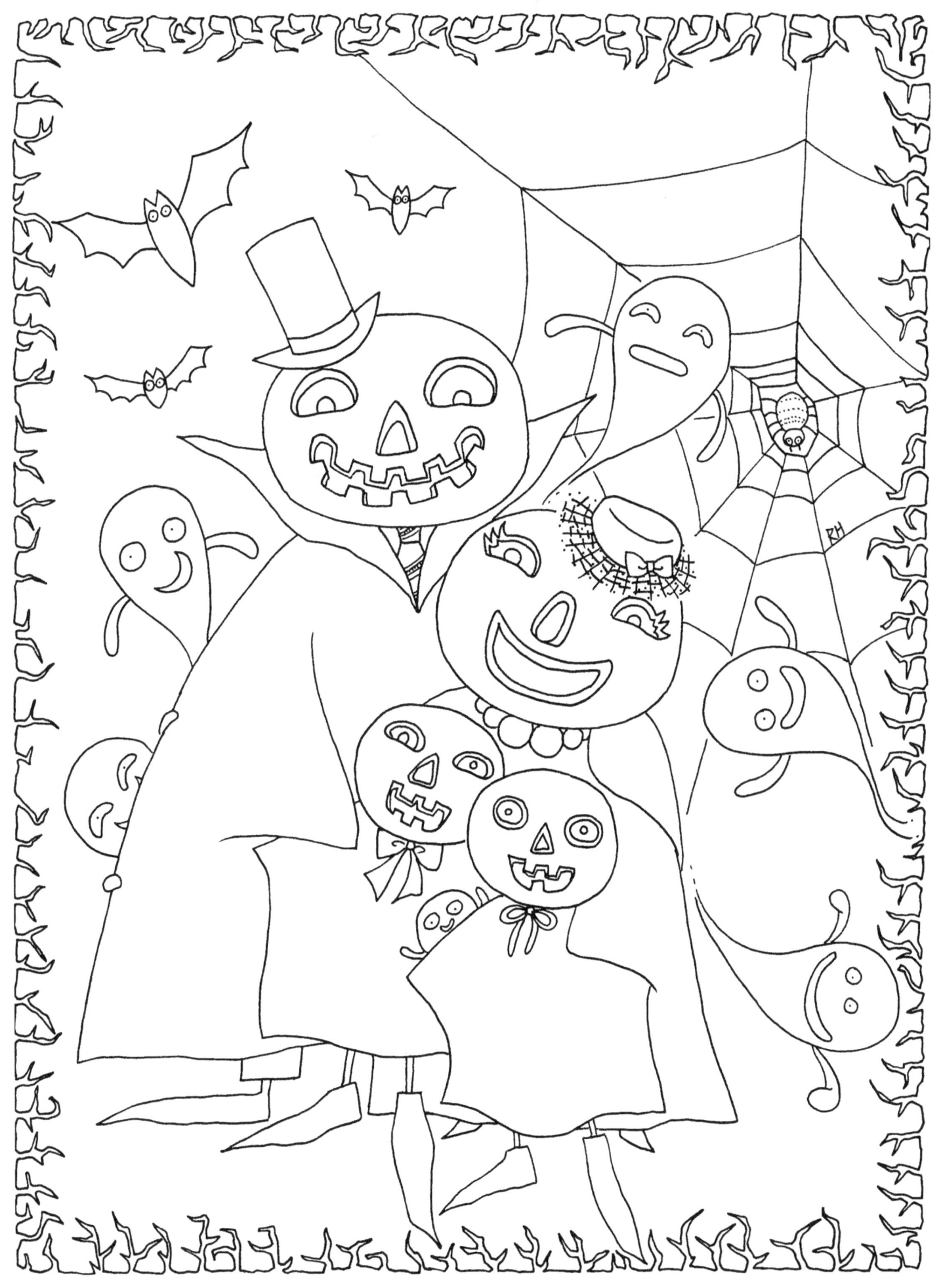

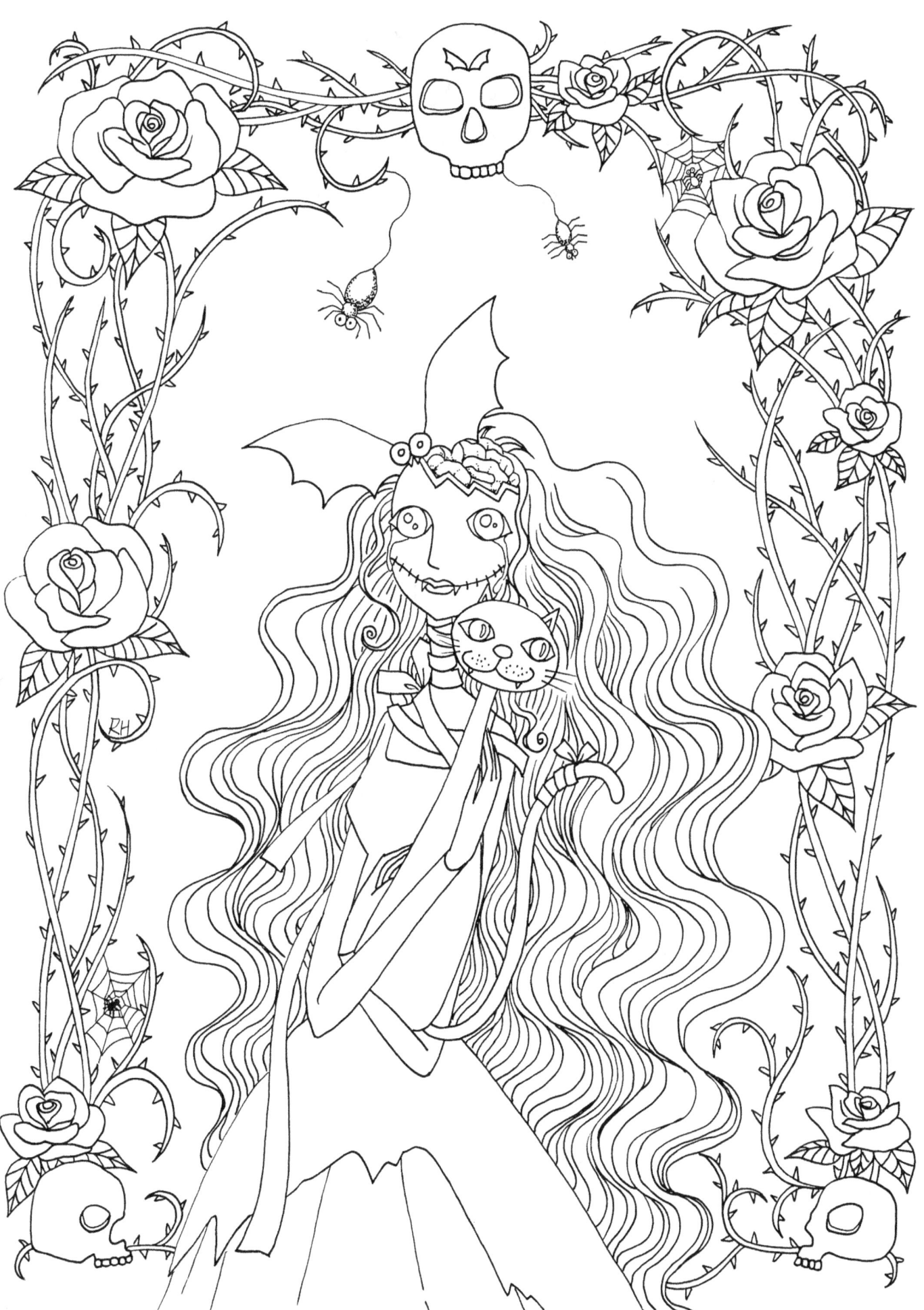

Contributing Artist
Wen Kung
Taiwan

Facebook : Wen's Zentangle life

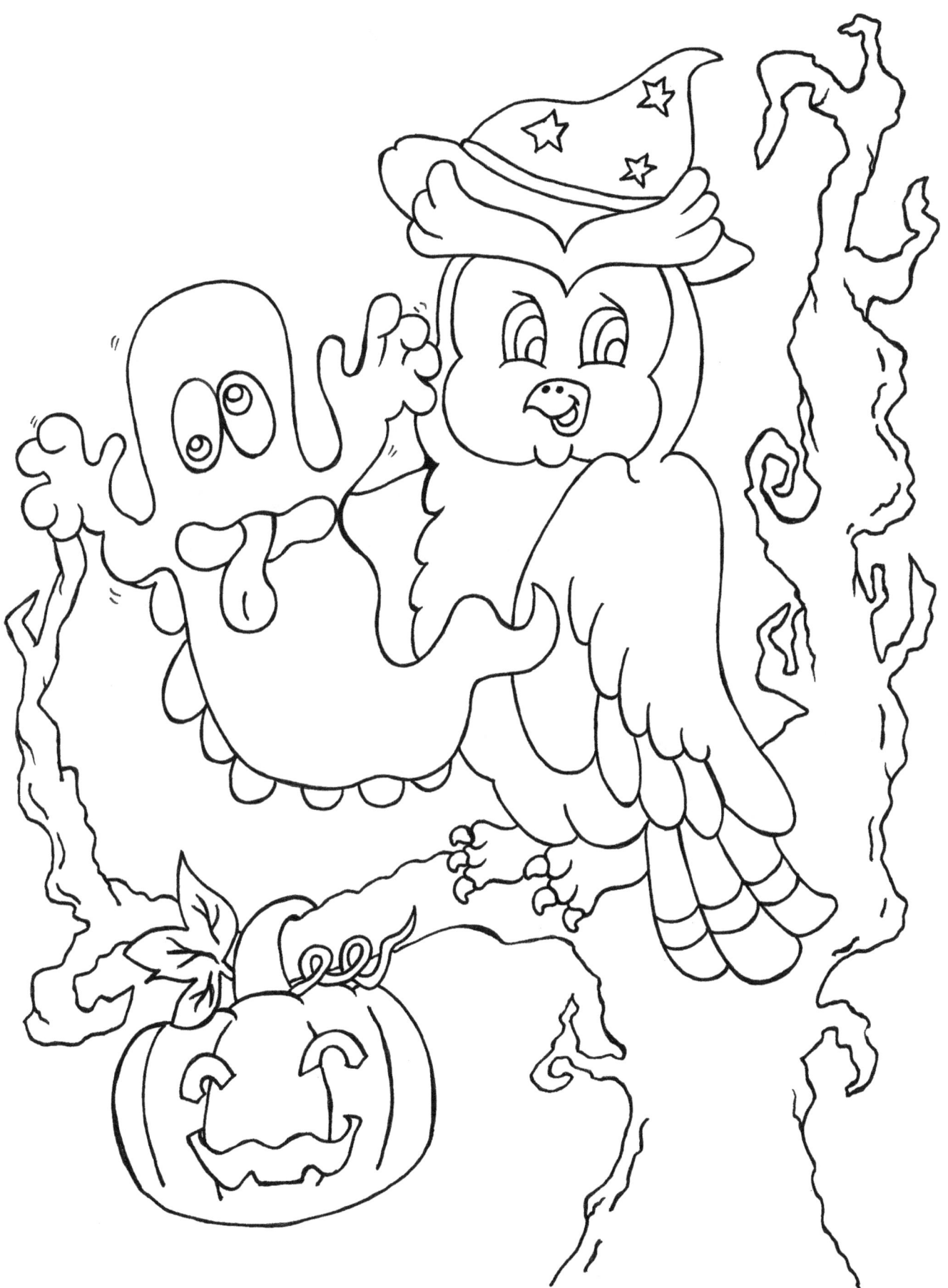

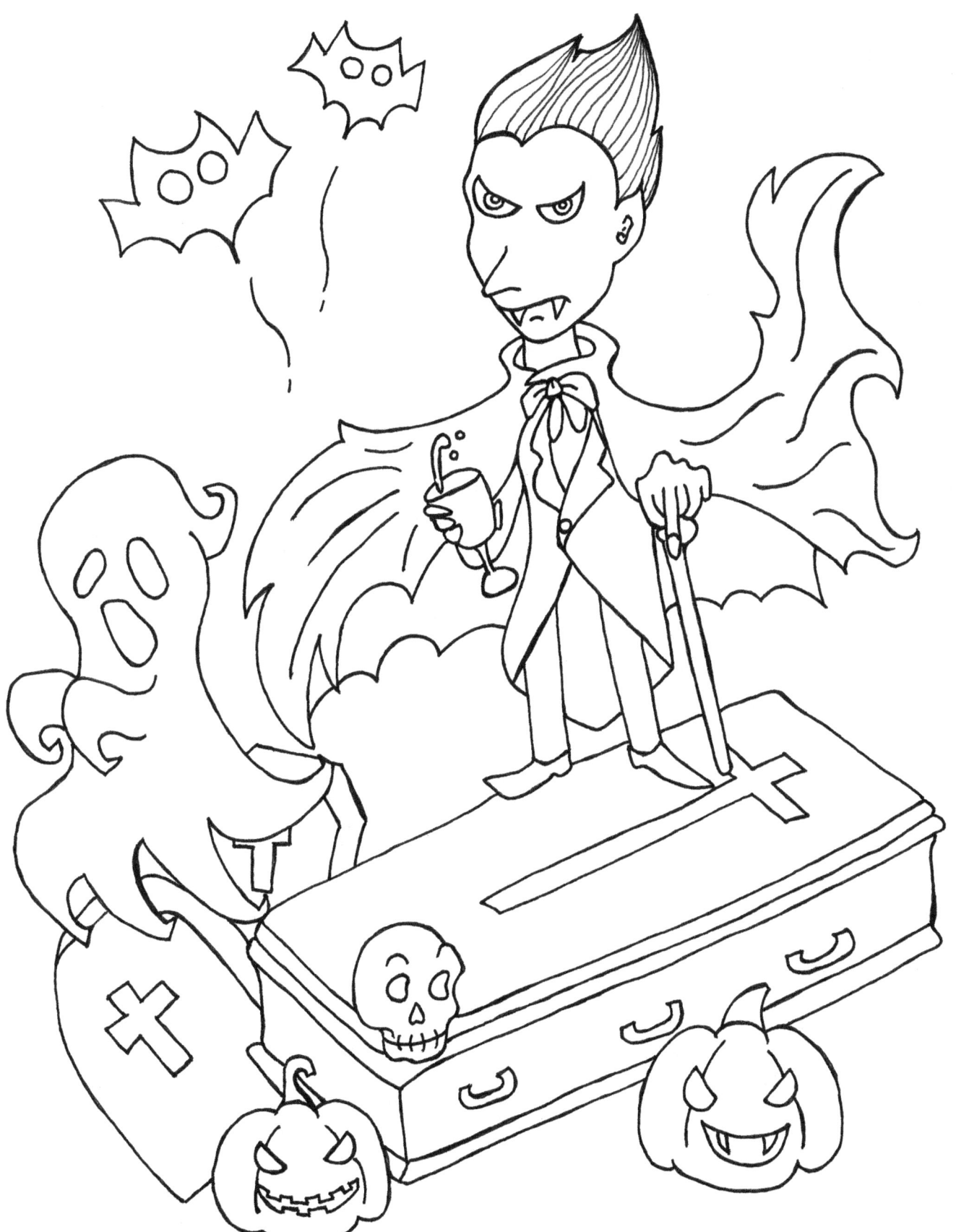

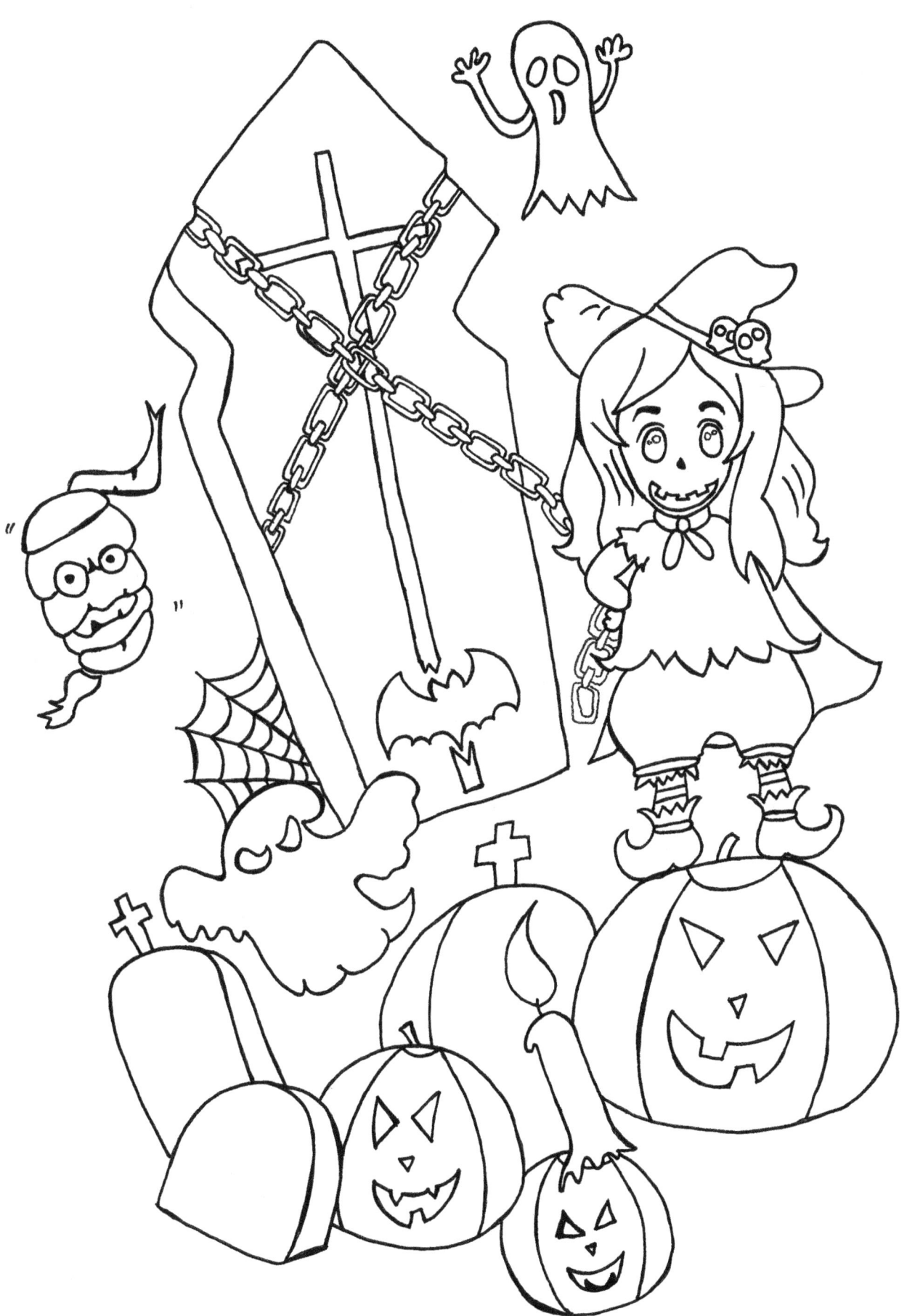

Test Your Colors here ....
Charts from "My Pocket Color Companion"
and
" My Color Companion"

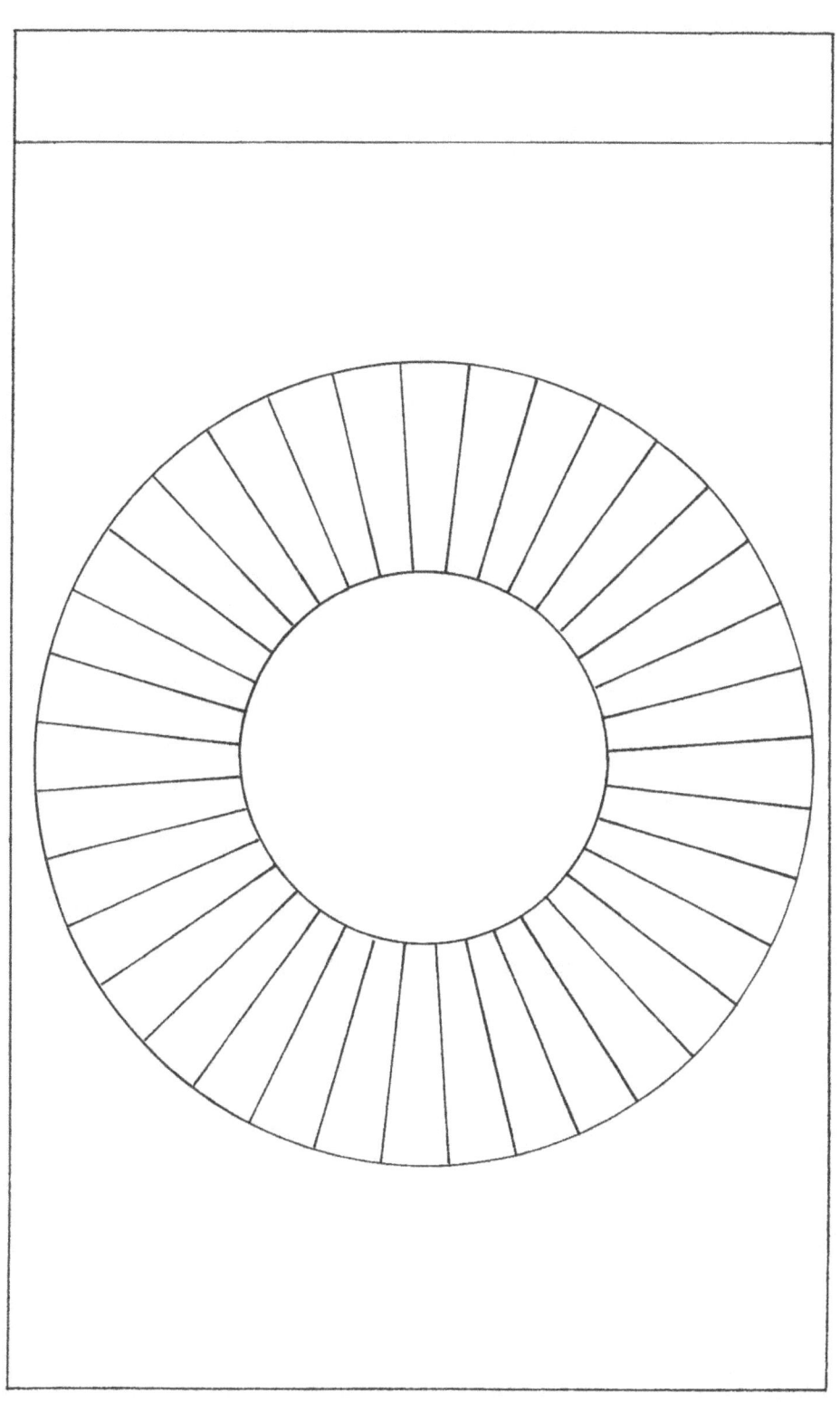

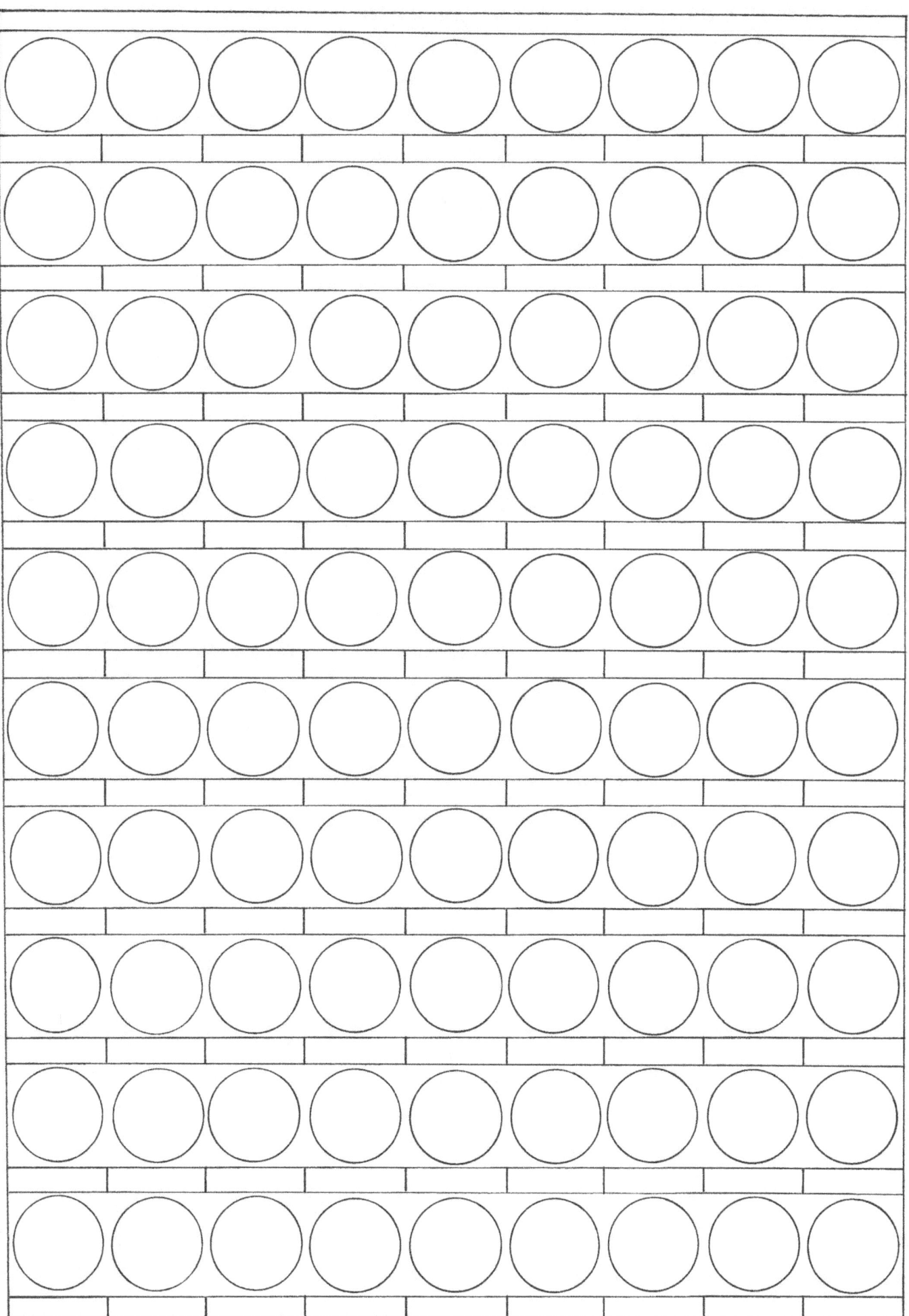

*...Also be sure
to check out
Halloween Cllections
Volume 1 and 2*

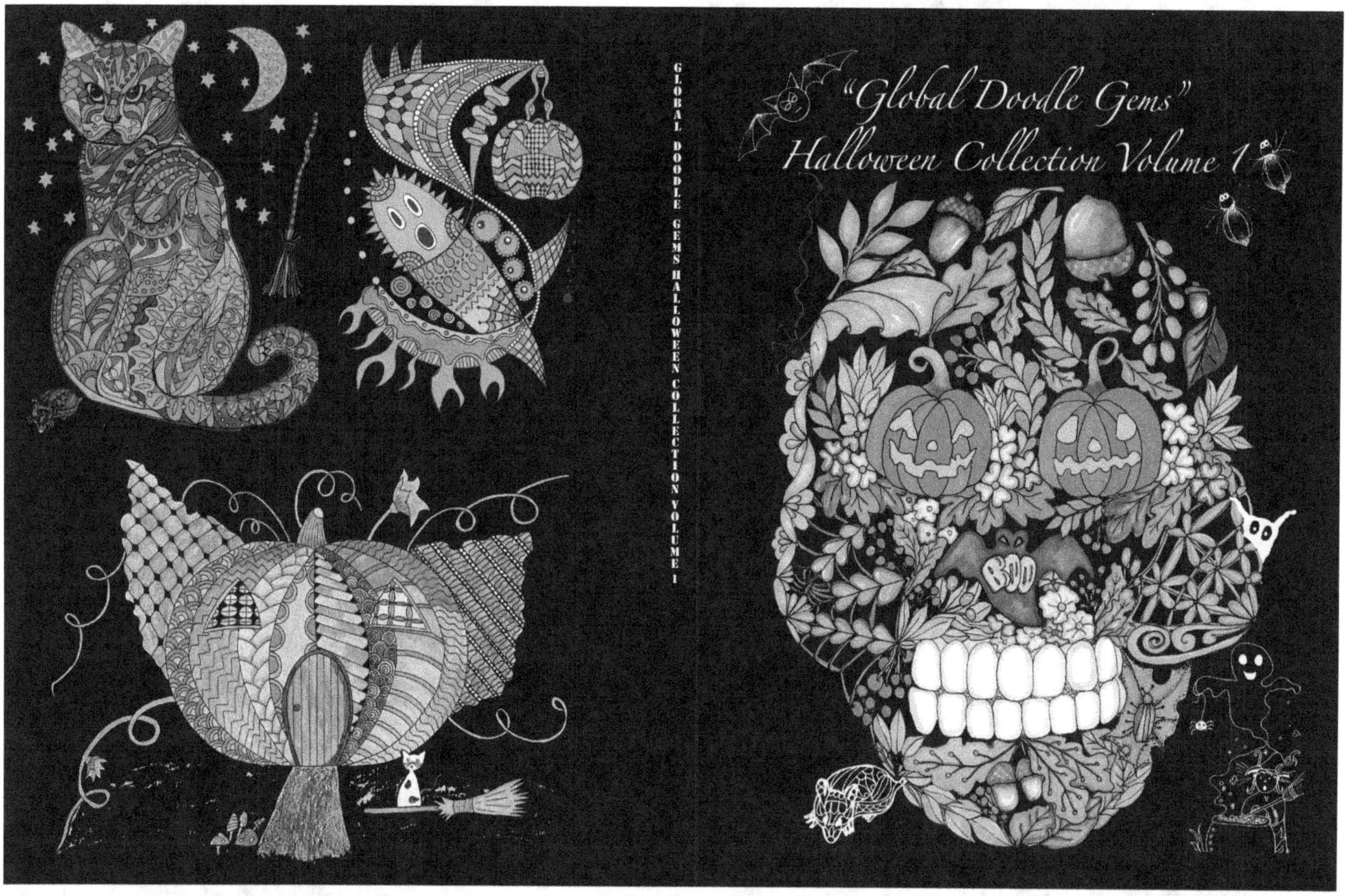

"Global Doodle Gems" Halloween Collection Volume 1

GLOBAL DOODLE GEMS HALLOWEEN COLLECTION VOLUME 1

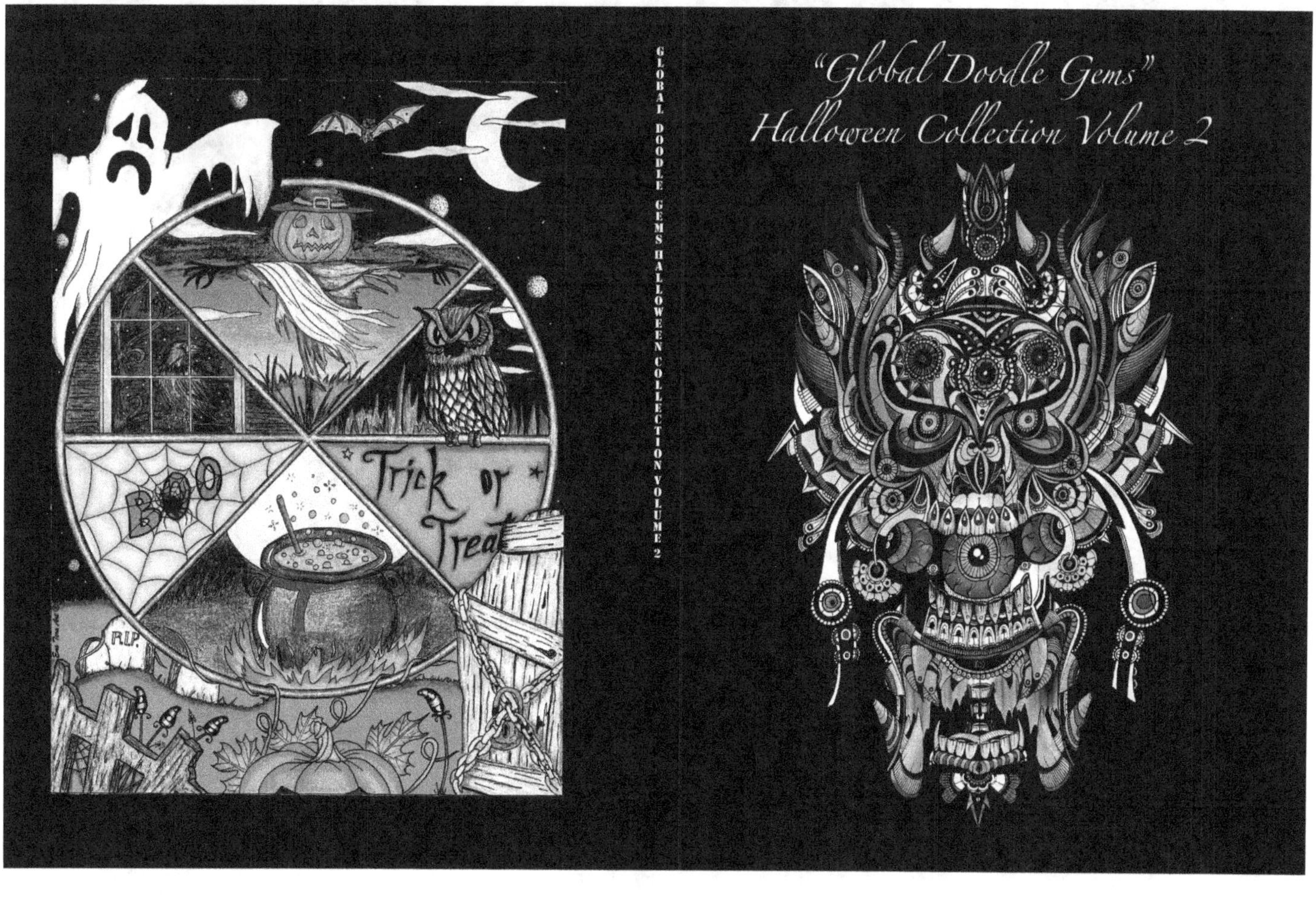

"Global Doodle Gems" Halloween Collection Volume 2

GLOBAL DOODLE GEMS HALLOWEEN COLLECTION VOLUME 2

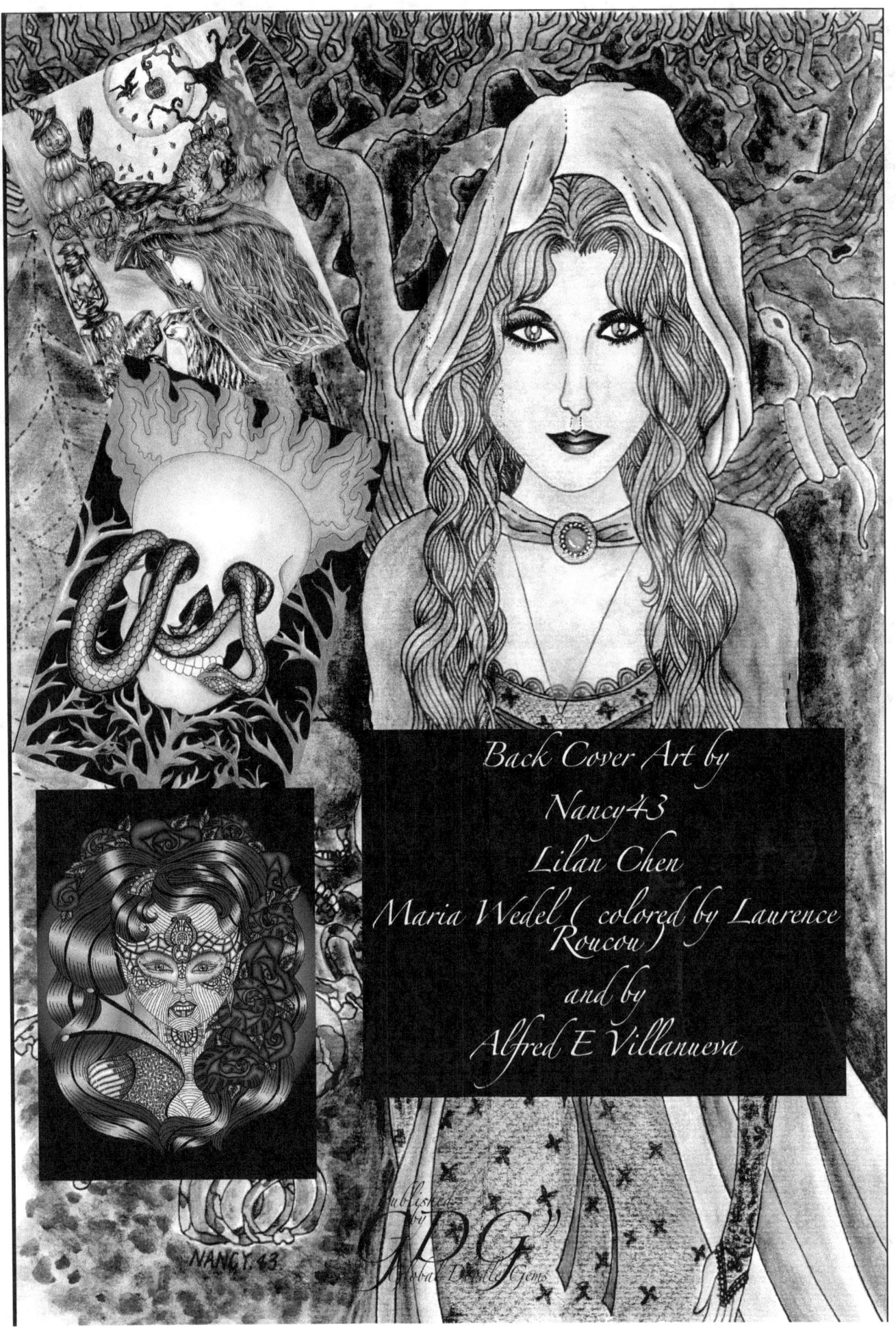

Back Cover Art by
Nancy43
Lilan Chen
Maria Wedel (colored by Laurence Roucou)
and by
Alfred E Villanueva